INTO
THE HEART
OF
AFRICA

Into the Heart of Africa is published in conjunction with
the exhibition of the same name, which will be on view at
the Royal Ontario Museum, Toronto, from
16 November 1989 to 6 August 1990.
The exhibition will then travel to
the Canadian Museum of Civilization (summer 1991),
the Vancouver Museum (fall 1991),
the Natural History Museum of
Los Angeles County (spring 1992),
and the Albuquerque Museum (summer 1992).

Into the Heart of Africa is organized and circulated by
the Royal Ontario Museum, Toronto, Canada,
with the generous support of
Imperial Oil Limited and Nabisco Brands Ltd, Canada.

The Royal Ontario Museum gratefully acknowledges
the financial assistance of the Ontario
Ministry of Citizenship—Multiculturalism Strategy.

The Royal Ontario Museum is an agency of
the Ontario Ministry of Culture and Communications.

INTO THE HEART OF AFRICA

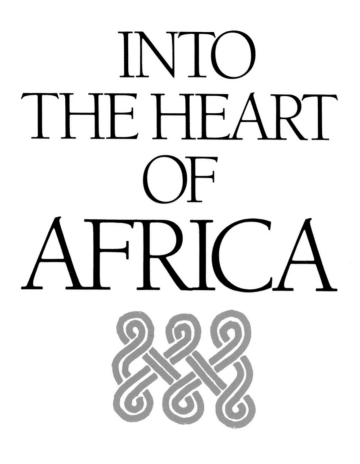

Jeanne Cannizzo

ROYAL ONTARIO MUSEUM
TORONTO

Canadian Cataloguing in Publication Data

Royal Ontario Museum.
    Into the heart of Africa

Catalogue to accompany an exhibition held Nov. 16,
1989–July 29, 1990 at the Museum.
Includes bibliographical references.
ISBN 0–88854–350–6

1. Art, African - Exhibitions. 2. Art, African -
Collectors and collecting - Ontario - History -
Exhibitions. 3. Royal Ontario Museum - Exhibitions.
I. Cannizzo, Jeanne, 1947–   . II. Title.

N7380.5.R69 1989   709'.6'0740113541   C89–094784–8

Cover: Detail of Mongo dancer from Zaire, photographed by the
Reverend A. W. Banfield probably sometime between 1915 and 1930.
(Photo: Department of Ethnology, ROM, gift of the A. W. Banfield
Estate)

Editing: Barbara Ibronyi
Design: Virginia Morin
Production: Lorna Hawrysh
Exhibition logo: Susan Nagy

Typesetting by Trigraph Inc.
Separations and halftones by Legg Bros. Graphics Limited
Printed and bound in Canada at General Printers

CONTENTS

ACKNOWLEDGEMENTS

My own journey through the exhibition and this book has been made both more exciting and easier by working with Brian Boyle, Jo Breyfogel, Arni Brownstone, Marianne Collins, Judith Cselenyi, Lory Drusian, Julia Fenn, David Fujiwara, Mary Hayes, Brian Hogarth, Margaret Anne Knowles, Helen Kilgour, Santiago Ku, Lynne Kurylo, Mostyn Lloyd, Julia Matthews, Allan McColl, Brian Musselwhite, Susan Nagy, Trudy Nicks, Pauline O'Brien, Rolf Seifert, Steven Spencer, and Margo Welch.

I am also most grateful to the following departments in the Royal Ontario Museum: Publication Services; the Office of the Associate Director, Exhibits; the Office of the Associate Director, Curatorial; the Public Relations Department; Exhibit Design Services; and the Library and Archives. Many thanks are also due to Edwin A. Goodman, the chairman of the Museum's Board of Trustees during the planning and organization of the exhibition.

Most of all I want to thank David A. T. Stafford, without whom I might never have gone to Africa, as well as the people of Sierra Leone, whose artful performances almost convinced me never to leave.

AFRICA

PEOPLES

1 Asante
2 Basotho
3 Chokwe
4 Edo
5 Hausa
6 Igbo
7 Kongo
8 Kota
9 Kuba
10 Lala
11 Lega
12 Lozi
13 Lunda
14 Lwena (Lovale)
15 Maasai
16 Mamvu
17 Mangbetu
18 Mende
19 Mongo
20 Ngbaka
21 Ngombe
22 Nupe
23 Ovimbundu
24 Sokoto Caliphate
25 Xhosa
26 Yombe
27 Yoruba
28 Zande
29 Zulu

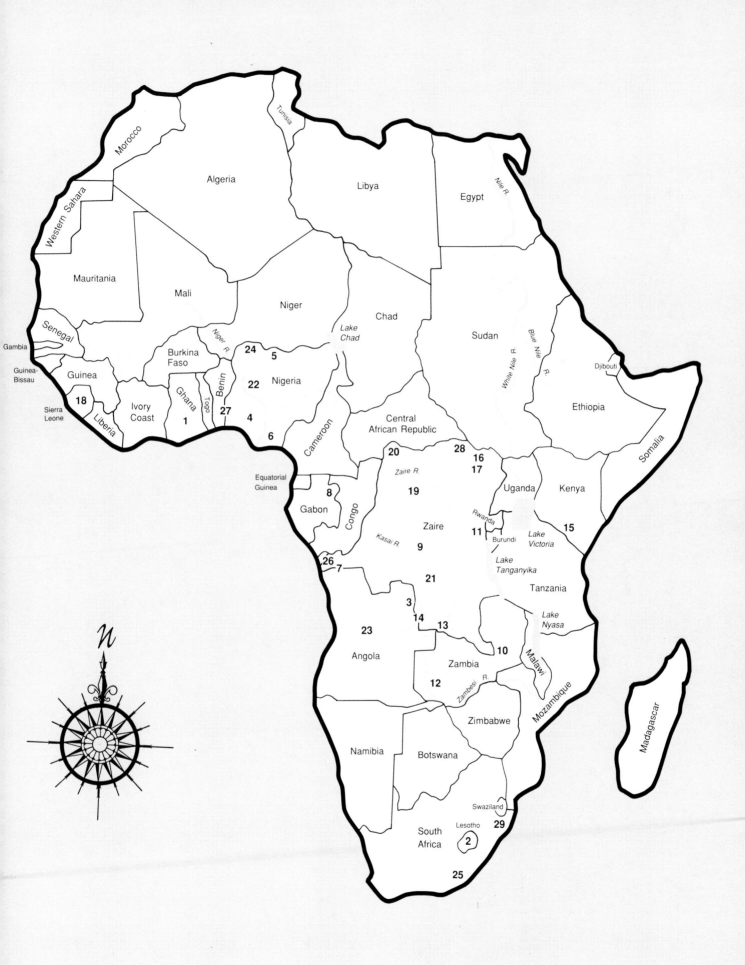

INTRODUCTION

Anthropology is frequently described as a kind of dialogue between the ethnographic other and the cultural self. This characterization is meant, among other things, to suggest the "fictional" nature of anthropology, for the work is generated in the interaction of the anthropologist's own cultural preconceptions and ideological assumptions with those of the people among whom he or she works. As such, the dialogue reveals something of the other as well as the self.

This description also conjures up the basic method of gathering anthropological data in the field: observing what people do, taking part when possible and appropriate, and talking with them about their beliefs and ideas. These were the kinds of conversations, or anthropological dialogues, I myself had in Sierra Leone, where I did research on children's street masquerades. But when I turned to the African collections of the Royal Ontario Museum, the people who had made and used the objects were no longer alive. Nor were the Canadian military men and missionaries who had collected the artifacts.

Yet as I spent hour upon hour in the Museum storeroom, those dialogues seemed to emerge from the masks, baskets, sculptures, and beadwork in which they had been embodied for generations. Such conversations may be conducted on many planes, across space and through time. An examination of this Epa mask from Nigeria provides the opportunity to try to hear a few of them.

The Yoruba speak with their own ancestors and culture heroes and to themselves through this kind of mask. During the Epa festival, held every two years between March and May, these masks perform to ensure the well-being of the community. Each mask is the property of a lineage group and marks memorable events in local history, drawing attention to outstanding village personalities. At the same time, the totality of the ritual performance, which often includes several masks, celebrates the cultural values to which the Yoruba as a nation subscribe.

The basic form consists of an elaborate superstructure borne by a helmet-mask with two faces, one on the front and the other on the back. The central male figure in this example wears a large magical hat and is flanked by representations of wrought iron staffs hung with bells and of antelope horns filled with medicine for procuring ritual power. Before him is a square divination board, its upper surface decorated with the face of Eshu, the deity who acts as an intermediary, bearing sacrifices to the gods.

These iconographic clues suggest that the figure is a priest of Osanyin, the god of herbal medicine, or an Ifa diviner. In everyday practice, the priests of Osanyin are not only powerful herbalists but healers of the psyche as well. Equally respected are the ritual practitioners who seek to use supernatural wisdom on behalf of their human clients, through the Ifa divination system.

The complete masquerade, with full costume and dance, might be considered a choreographed dialogue between the young men who wear the masks and the audience. In some communities the dancers are required to jump from a small earthmound with the heavy masks. If they lose their balance, they risk upsetting the harmony and prosperity of village life for a whole year. Their prowess celebrates the vitality of youth and the quickness of the living.

This sculpture also speaks of the master carver who made it emerge

Mask, Yoruba, Nigeria, probably carved in the 1930s. Wood, pigmentation. Height 118 cm. 989.130.1. Gift of the Titcombe family. (Photo: Santiago Ku)

from a single block of wood, from which he coaxed both the crudity of the dancer's helmet-mask and the refinement of the superstructure. According to John Picton, a Yoruba specialist, that artist may have been Bamgboye of Odo-Owa in the northeastern part of Yoruba territory. Born about 1888, he was known for his excellent craftsmanship and the complexity of his compositions. In any event, the artist has achieved a dynamic unity between individual expression, cultural continuity, and sculptural integrity, to produce an imposing work.

Finally, the mask represents a cross-cultural encounter, a conversation across cultural boundaries, for it was brought back to Canada by the Reverend Thomas Titcombe. As a young man he left England and settled in Hamilton, Ontario. In 1908 Titcombe joined the Sudan Interior Mission bound for Nigeria. There he worked among the Yagba (a Yoruba subgroup) for the next twenty-two years, until ill health forced his return home. It is not known from whom or exactly when he acquired this mask—whether during his long career or on one of two brief return visits in 1942/1943 and 1948/1949. He did tell his family, however, that it was presented to him by an "old witchdoctor" who had converted to Christianity. Titcombe kept the mask to remind him of his first days in the mission field and the experiences he shared with the Yagba, as their lives intertwined in colonial Nigeria.

The life history of this mask—from ritual object to missionary souvenir and finally to museum specimen—illustrates the transformational power of context and suggests that the meaning and significance of an object change according to the circumstances in which it appears and is understood. That transformational power is particularly evident in museums, which, like anthropology, are also essentially "fictional" in their nature. The meaning of their collections is generated in the interaction between the curator, the object, and the visitor. As such negotiated realities, museums are crucial to understanding one's cultural self as well as the ethnographic other.

A Yagba family from the Nigerian town of Egbe, photographed by the Reverend Thomas Titcombe in the early part of the 20th century. (Photo: Courtesy of the Titcombe family)

"Women carrying water for the building of new Egbe Church," a photograph from Titcombe's album, which was taken in Nigeria in the early 20th century. (Photo: Courtesy of the Titcombe family)

THE IMPERIAL CONNECTION

Queen Victoria's jubilee in 1897, marking her sixty years on the throne, was extravagantly celebrated at home and throughout her empire. Canada, as part of that empire, had horizons that were much broader than those defined by its own political boundaries. Nor were Canadians marginal participants in the empire's triumphs and defeats. As British subjects, they took an active part in all the opportunities an imperial power had to offer individuals in the dominions.

According to historian James Morris, in his book *Pax Britannica,* in that jubilee year

> there was no exact dividing line between a Canadian Briton and a British Briton. Their accents were diverging it is true, but they carried the same passports and usually honoured the same ideals.... Hundreds of thousands of British Canadians regarded the imperial saga as part of their own national heritage. The excitement of the New Imperialism was almost as intense in Toronto as it was in London. (P. 391)

Stamp issued 7 December 1898 to commemorate the inauguration of imperial penny postage. (Photo: Reproduced courtesy of Canada Post Corporation)

Major General Sir Garnet Wolseley, at the time of the Asante campaign in 1874. *The Illustrated London News,* 28 March 1874.

Some of that excitement was generated through the popular adoration of the heroes of the age. The perfect British soldier was personified in Major General Sir Garnet Wolseley. Idolized by the public, he fought throughout the empire. His career as an imperial commander saw him leading the Red River expedition against the métis in western Canada in 1870, capturing the capital of the Asante kingdom in West Africa in 1874, and overseeing the subjugation of the Zulu state in South Africa in 1879.

Of equal renown was the Scottish missionary explorer Dr. David Livingstone, the first European to see the thundering Victoria Falls on the Zambezi River and several of the great lakes of eastern and central Africa. His exploits during his thirty years on the continent thrilled the English-speaking world and inspired several generations of Canadian missionaries to venture into the interior. Their vision, like his, was to replace "paganism" with Christianity, the slave trade with legitimate commerce, and

Taken in 1874 from Kumase, the capital of the Asante kingdom, this gold necklace was described in an early catalogue entry as part of the spoils of war belonging to Wolseley. After his return to England, he presented it to a family friend, whose descendants sold it to a benefactor of the Royal Ontario Museum.

Necklace, Asante, Ghana, 19th century. Gold. Length 52 cm. HA1266. Gift of Mrs. George A. Sweny. (Photo: Santiago Ku)

"barbarous" customs with their own form of civilization. Seeking glory on spiritual battlefields no less dangerous than the secular ones where Canadian soldiers fought, many of them paid with their health and lives for their beliefs.

Encountering unfamiliar cultures with worldviews radically different from their own, those soldiers and missionaries who returned home brought back many souvenirs and trophies of their journeys into the heart of Africa.

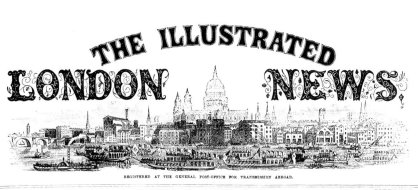

No. 1804.—VOL. LXIV.   SATURDAY, MARCH 21, 1874.   WITH EXTRA SUPPLEMENT | SIXPENCE. | By Post, 6½d.

European troops entering Kumase. *The Illustrated London News,* 21 March 1874.

Dr. David Livingstone. *Heroes of the Dark Continent* by J. W. Buel.

Livingstone's discovery of Lake Nyasa. *Heroes of the Dark Continent* by J. W. Buel.

The missionaries desperately wanted to destroy the trade in what was sometimes called "black ivory" and so to heal what they thought of as Africa's "open sore." These slave whips were collected in Angola by the Reverend Wilberforce Lee of Cowansville, Quebec.

Whips, Ovimbundu, Angola, collected 1889–1895. Hide. *Top to bottom:* lengths 83 cm, 99 cm. 973.325.22, 973.325.23. Gift of Miss Dorothea Bell. (Photo: Santiago Ku)

FOR CROWN AND EMPIRE

The call to serve the empire sounded loudly in the ears of Canadian soldiers, some of whom fought in the "savage little wars" that so marked the closing years of the 19th century and the beginning of the 20th. Campaigning against African peoples who resisted the imperial advance and sometimes against rival European powers, these soldiers sought to extend the Pax Britannica throughout the African colonies claimed by the United Kingdom.

"Britain's Bulwarks," imperial forces, 1898. (Photo: Courtesy of the Director, National Army Museum, London, England)

CAPTAIN JOHN F. CREAN
IMPERIAL OFFICER

One of those who fought for Crown and Empire was John F. Crean of Toronto. Born in 1858, he joined the Queen's Own Rifles when he was eighteen, eventually becoming sergeant major. A professional soldier all his life, he took part in the campaign against the métis in western Canada during the uprising of 1885. Later, with the Gold Coast Regiment of the West African Frontier Force, he led a contingent of Hausa soldiers in Ghana.

The Hausa are an Islamicized people living in northern Nigeria, well known as both long-distance traders and soldiers. Under the direction of British officers, they were widely used as infantry throughout the colonies of West Africa. Together Crean and his troops took part in the Asante War of 1900.

The Asante lived in one of the most powerful states in West Africa. A wealthy trading empire and political confederacy, the Asante kingdom had come into conflict with the British throughout the 19th century. Having suffered a major military defeat in 1874 and the exile of their king in 1896, the Asante rose again in 1900, after the governor of the British Crown Colony of the Gold Coast (now part of Ghana) tried to take possession of the Golden Stool, which enshrined the soul of the nation. A symbolic rather than utilitarian object, it was never actually sat upon. Colonial authorities were unsuccessful in their attempt to take the stool, but the Asante confederacy ceased to exist after the campaign of 1900 until it was restored in 1935.

GOLDEN STOOL CAUSES RISING.

Governor of Gold Coast Tried to Get the Sacred Emblem.

ALL THE TRIBES ARE IN ARMS.

Coomassie Runner Reports That of All the Chiefs Only King of Bekwai Remains Loyal.

Accra, British Gold Coast, Africa, April 6.—The situation in Ashanti is unchanged. A Coomassie runner reports that all the Ashanti tribes are in arms, the King of Bekwai alone remaining loyal.

Headline and introduction to an article on the Anglo-Asante War of 1900. Toronto *Daily Mail and Empire,* 9 April 1900. (Photo: Library of the University of Toronto)

John F. Crean as a young man in the Queen's Own Rifles. (Photo: Archives of Ontario)

Captain John F. Crean and Hausa soldiers, First Battalion, Gold Coast Regiment, about 1902 in Ghana. (Photo: Courtesy of John Gale Crean)

An artillery officer during operations against the Asante, Crean was mentioned in dispatches. He retired from service in Africa, possibly because of ill health, to accept an appointment in the Royal Canadian Artillery. Crean was a well-known sportsman and had once been a champion lightweight boxer, but when he died in 1907 the Toronto *Daily Mail and Empire* of 25 March noted in an obituary headed "West African Experience Proves Fatal" that "the torrid climate, every breath of which seems laden with poison for the European, completely wrecked his once robust constitution." Such a fate was not uncommon for those Canadians who travelled overseas in search of what they thought of as adventure, glory, a worthy vocation, or a promising career.

While in Africa, Crean gathered a substantial collection, but left no account of his activities. It is unknown if his Asante artifacts were spoils of war or acquisitions from the followers of the chief of Bekwae, an Asante ruler who chose to ally himself with the British and whose photograph appears in one of Crean's albums. Not surprisingly, Crean also brought home objects from the Africans he commanded. His Hausa collection, heavily weighted in favour of weapons, clearly reflects that people's military reputation.

One of Crean's helmets for use in West Africa is displayed with some of his Asante artifacts. The stool, carved from a single piece of wood, was probably for domestic rather than ceremonial use. Crean believed that the drum belonged to a chief and was used during war.

Left to right:
Stool, Asante, Ghana, collected c. 1900. Wood. Height 33 cm. HA1990. On loan from the Royal Canadian Military Institute, Toronto.
Helmet, England, c. 1900. Cloth, leather, wood. Height 21 cm. 989.138.3. Gift of Mr. John Gale Crean.
Drum, Asante, Ghana, collected c. 1900. Wood, skin, fibres. Height 55 cm. HA2040. On loan from the Royal Canadian Military Institute, Toronto.
(Photo: Santiago Ku)

Pipes, like the one illustrated, are carved rather than moulded and were sometimes used by the Asante as grave offerings. The figure is making a begging gesture, which is also associated with mourning. The small Hausa purse was used for carrying the Quran, the sacred text of Islam.

Tobacco pipe, Asante, Ghana, collected c. 1900. Fired clay, pigmentation. Height 7.6 cm. HA1984.
Quran pouch, Hausa, Nigeria, collected c. 1900. Leather. Length of pouch 10 cm. HA1974.
On loan from the Royal Canadian Military Institute, Toronto. (Photo: Santiago Ku)

22 Cloth does more than cover the body or soften the bed. It can reveal cultural origins, rank or social standing, gender, and sometimes age. The colour, texture, and volume of cloth can add to the vitality of many public occasions and to the intensity of more secluded events. This Asante cloth from southern Ghana, collected by Crean in 1900, was intended as a garment, probably for a man.

Textiles were closely linked to social and political hierarchies in this area. Thus royal and chiefly cloth were of highly valued silk, while textiles for commoners were more often of cotton. This piece is of cotton and was made by a male weaver using a horizontal double heddle loom. The narrow cloth strips produced on such a loom are then sewn together to form the cloth.

Detail of cloth, Asante, Ghana, collected c. 1900. Cotton, wool(?). Total length 218 cm. HA1995. On loan from the Royal Canadian Military Institute, Toronto. (Photo: Santiago Ku)

The Hausa have been well known for many generations as expert leather workers. The decorated leather on these objects is probably tanned goatskin.

Knives and sheaths, Hausa, Nigeria, collected c. 1900.
Top to bottom:
Iron, tin, brass, wood, leather, pigmentation. Length of sheath 27 cm, length of
knife 40 cm. HA1949a–b.
Iron, wood, leather, pigmentation. Length of knife 38 cm, length of sheath 26 cm.
HA1954a–b.
On loan from the Royal Canadian Military Institute, Toronto. (Photo:
Santiago Ku)

Objects, like people, have life histories. But this four-headed figure remains something of a mystery. It was collected by Gore Munbee Barrow, who died the principal of a boys' school in the quiet Ontario town of Grimsby. As a young man, however, he was an officer in the imperial army. He fought in the Transvaal during the Boer War and by 1902 was a lieutenant in the West African Frontier Force. The next year he took part in the British campaign against the Sokoto Caliphate, an Islamic state in northern Nigeria.

Somewhere in Nigeria he acquired this statue. It was almost certainly made by an Igbo artist about the turn of the century in a village in the southeastern part of the country and probably depicts a spirit or supernatural being. A white face is found on many representations of Igbo deities and is often interpreted as an indication of moral purity.

Many years later Barrow's family gave the statue to the Royal Ontario Museum. They believed that one of his men had been sacrificed to this "death fetish." The inscription "No. 80, Lagos, W.A.F.F." on the metal tag that accompanied the figure was thought to be the victim's military identification.

Historical archives have not revealed reports of such an event. Whether or not the story is accurate, the alleged barbarity of "savage customs" often attracted collectors to certain kinds of artifacts, which now fill our museums.

Figure, Igbo, Nigeria, late 19th century. Wood, pigmentation, metal, glass. Height 42 cm. 962.76.5/7. Gift of the Reverend O. G. Barrow. (Photo: Santiago Ku)

LIEUTENANT FREDERICK HAMILTON
WAR CORRESPONDENT

The imperial sentiments of anglophone Canadians were highly aroused by the outbreak of the Boer War in 1899. Canadian security was not threatened by this South African war between Britain and the Boer republics of Transvaal and the Orange Free State, but demands, especially from Ontario, for Canada to support the Crown led to the dispatch of the 1000-strong Royal Canadian Regiment. A later contingent and those who enlisted individually in the British army brought the number of Canadians who took part in the war to some 7300.

In their initial engagement at the battle of Paardeberg in 1900, Canadian forces were instrumental in effecting the surrender of the Afrikaners under General Piet Arnoldus Cronje. Those exploits on the distant front were covered for the public back home by several war correspondents.

"From Canada's Snows to Afric's Sunny Fountains," troops departing Ottawa for the Boer War in South Africa. *The Illustrated London News,* 10 February 1900.

CANADIANS AT DE AAR.

Mr. Frederick Hamilton Tells How Sunday, Dec. 3, Was Spent.

BLINDING, SCORCHING DUST

Not a Pleasant Picture of the Climatic Conditions of the Great British Camping Ground—Otherwise the Canadian Battalion Was Alright—The Boys Under Canvas and Expecting Marching Order: Hourly—Two Million Pounds of Munitions of War at De Aar—South African Scenery Contrasted With Canadian—A Splendid Night Scene

THE CANADIANS AT PAARDEBERG.

Graphic Story of the Battle by Mr. Frederick Hamilton.

FIRST COMPLETE NARRATIVE.

The Week of Heavy Marching That Preceded the Battle—Night After Night Spent Tramping the Veldt—The Sudden Call to Arms on Sunday Morning, Feb. 18—Across the Modder River—A Description of the Boer Position—Its Advantages and Disadvantages—Battle Strength of the Royal Canadians—Officers Actually in Charge

Headlines and introductions for two of Hamilton's reports from South Africa. Toronto *Globe,* 8 January, 6 April 1900. (Photo: Library of the University of Toronto)

Lieutenant Frederick Hamilton reported for the Toronto *Globe* and was the first to break the news of the victory at Paardeberg. When not recording events on the battlefield, visiting the wounded in hospital, or covering life in camp, Hamilton collected artifacts at the request of David Boyle, curator of the ethnology and archaeology collections of the Ontario Provincial Museum in Toronto. An article by Hamilton in the Ontario *Archaeological Report* of 1900 recounts how his strange commission came about.

> Mr. Boyle wrote to me after I had landed in South Africa suggesting that I get for him any information, or any objects of interest (not mere curiosities) from an ethnological point of view, and it fell out that very soon after receiving his letter my travels brought me near numerous native kraals. His remarks had quickened my interest in a people whom I found amiable, amusing and interesting, and I purchased from them what household objects I could carry, and from time to time noted down such details as I observed of their domestic habits. The entirely fragmentary nature of my observations are apparent. (P. 40)

Predictably, the small collection he managed to assemble is as fragmentary as the journal entries recorded in his article. The light that his notes throw on the actual process of collecting, however, enhances the historical and ethnological value of the artifacts.

The beer strainer illustrated was in use when Hamilton bought it and another one in a large Basotho village near Vereeniging in the Orange Free State at the end of May 1900. He noted the following:

> These things were made of a small wiry reed which grows by streams.…The two strainers are of differing patterns and it is important to remember that I bought them in the same village, from the same people so far as I can recall. A woman with her hair 'done up' in straight tuffs, with bits of grass for curl-papers, acted as intermediary, as she knew a little English and had the requisite size, lungs and chest. When the buying languished she cooly demanded her 'percel', i.e. percentage-commission. I was amused.…(P. 44)

His notes on this child's skirt are much shorter:

> Bought at a Basuto [Basotho] kraal near Winburg a small girl's dress. (P. 42)

His account of this nosecleaner reveals not only something of his own personality but also one of the main reasons that these people gave up their objects, namely the need for money to participate in a growing cash economy. Hamilton was probably unaware of the pejorative connotations of the word "Kaffir," which came originally from the Arabic word for unbeliever or infidel.

> 26th May Bought to-day at a kraal near Wonderpan, about twenty miles south of Kroomstadt, the 'Kaffir handkerchief' from an old Basuto woman. This implement (whose use I dimly recollect having seen alluded to by some African traveller, I believe Livingstone) is a small arrowheaded pewter implement about 4½ inches long.…This

is used by the old people alone. The natives regarded my desire to own this as a huge joke.

Attached to this implement was the circular brass blanket buckle....No distinction of sex is made in the use either of this implement or the 'handkerchief'....The old woman who was the owner was reluctant to give it up but found three shillings enough to induce her to part with it. (P. 43)

Awarded a South African campaign medal, Hamilton returned to Canada, where he remained an ardent imperialist who favoured the appointment of a British prince as the king of Canada.

Left to right:
Child's skirt, Basotho, Lesotho, collected 1900. Fibre cord, leather, beads. Length 40 cm. 22125.
Nose cleaner, Basotho, Lesotho, collected 1900. Metal, beads, leather. Length 40 cm. 22109.
Beer strainer, Basotho, Lesotho, collected 1900. Woven plant fibre. Length 51 cm. 22112.
(Photo: Santiago Ku)

Another veteran of the Boer War was Edward Mountjoy Pearse, a surgeon who served with a British army medical unit in South Africa, where he collected some thirty pieces of Zulu beadwork. Unfortunately, he recorded virtually no information about them, so that their exact function and use is unknown. In general, Zulu beadwork is for personal adornment. Made only by girls and women, it is worn by both sexes.

This particular necklace probably acted as a love message sent from a young woman to a man, who then incorporated it into his courting attire. Wearing the necklace was a public statement that he had established a relationship with the maker of the beadwork gift. The colours of the beads and the way they were arranged determined the specific meaning, which can no longer be precisely decoded. However, depending on its placement in the design, the colour blue can suggest either fidelity or ill feeling and can signal a request. Red, the colour of fire and blood, conveys strong emotion—whether anger, love, or longing. White generally speaks of purity and goodness.

Necklace, Zulu, South Africa, collected 1900. Beads, fibre. Length of panel 10 cm. 971.119.7. Gift of Mr. Allan T. H. Pearse. (Photo: Santiago Ku)

The struggles of the European powers in World War I were played out not only in the trenches of the Western Front but also in the grassfields of Central Africa. This stool was part of the spoils of war taken by British forces in 1915 from Government House at Buea, in the German colony of Kamerun (now Cameroon).

The stool is probably a piece of contact art created in the interaction between Africans and Europeans in the early part of this century. In the style of the western grassfields, it displays some indigenous features, including its round form. At each side is an attendant riding a leopard, the royal alter ego. The male attendant on the left may be holding a chiefly drinking horn, while the female carries what looks like a gourd, which some scholars have suggested might contain palm wine. The latticework back is composed of highly stylized frogs, which are symbols of fertility, or spiders, which signify wisdom to those who know how to read the traditional designs.

Other features may have been modified to meet European expectations or suggested by non-African forms. For example, the two attendants and the latticework back make the stool more like an armchair. There are also some iconographic changes: leopards would not normally appear in pairs, nor in association with women. The stool may well have been a gift from an African ruler to a German colonial officer or an elaborate piece of tourist art bought by a European.

Prestige stool, Grassfields, Cameroon, collected 1915. Wood, pigmentation. Height 100 cm. 949.84.4. Gift of Mr. James Somerville. (Photo: ROM)

IN LIVINGSTONE'S FOOTSTEPS

Taking Dr. David Livingstone as their model and inspiration, Christian missionaries from all parts of the British Empire believed that they were bringing "light" to the "Dark Continent." That light was to transform the lives of their converts.

Several different Protestant denominations sent missionaries into Africa. Although there were many doctrinal differences among the evangelists, there seems to have been only one basic model of what they thought an African Christian should be. To convert meant first of all to give up previous religious beliefs and rituals. It also meant to subscribe not only to Christianity but to conform to European customs. While this model was an abstract view applied indiscriminately and rarely moderated by existing cultural practices, there were considerable differences in the reactions of individual missionaries to the peoples they met. The responses of those peoples were equally varied: many missionaries were tolerated, some seem to have been genuinely liked, and a few were actively discouraged from preaching and completely rejected. The educational opportunities, medical clinics, and knowledge of the wider world that the missionaries offered were, however, often readily recognized.

Mrs. Thomas Titcombe offering "a lesson in how to wash clothes" to Yagba women in northern Nigeria about 1915. (Photo: Courtesy of the Titcombe family)

DARKEST AFRICA

AREA, 12,000,000 SQ.MI.   POPULATION, 150,000,000.

Areas in white repre-
sent territory occupied
by Mission Stations or
Christian communities.
Area in black shows
the unevangelized por-
tion of the continent.

Africa as seen by Canadian missionaries in 1904. *The Story of
Chisamba*, by H. W. Barker.

The original catalogue entry for this hat, collected by the Reverend Walter T.
Currie in Angola, describes it as "a grass hat made by a native in imitation of a
white man's straw hat." The rope was made in Angola at the Chisamba mission
station run by Canadian Congregational missionaries. Martha Wightman, a
volunteer working in the field, brought it back to Canada.

Rope, Ovimbundu, Angola, collected 1917–1920. Hemp. Diameter 10 cm. HA618.
Gift of Miss Martha Wightman.
Hat, Ovimbundu, Angola, collected 1886–1910. Grass. Height 6.4 cm, diameter 24
cm. HAC191. Gift of Mrs. Walter Thomas Currie.
(Photo: Santiago Ku)

32 A group of mission school boys in Angola in 1910. (Photo: The United Church of Canada/Victoria University Archives, Toronto)

Mennonite Brethren church in a Nupe village in Nigeria about 1903. (Photo: SIM, International)

THE REVEREND WALTER T. CURRIE
CANADA'S LIVINGSTONE

"We turn our backs on the last traces of civilization and our faces toward the centre of the Dark Continent," wrote Walter T. Currie in a letter home upon his arrival in Angola.

Currie was born in 1858 into a middle class Toronto family already interested in the abolition of slavery. As a boy he read and reread Livingstone's journals. He seems to have decided at quite an early age to become a missionary. In 1886, after completing a course at the Congregational Church training school in Montreal, he left for the Portuguese colony of Angola with his new bride. She was dead of fever in six weeks, but he was to live in Central Africa for the next twenty-five years.

He established his base at Chisamba among the Ovimbundu, who had been active intermediaries in the slave trade in central Angola for centuries. They also controlled the rubber trade from the late 19th century until its collapse in 1911, the same year that the slave trade was finally ended. Currie envisaged his converts carrying the gospel into the interior with their caravans, which travelled where no mission stations existed. At the same time, he wanted to provide alternative employment to his male converts, because he saw the life of a carrier on the trail as "full of temptations."

The Reverend Walter T. Currie as a
young man. *The Story of Chisamba,*
by H. W. Barker.

34

Currie's carpentry workshop at Chisamba mission station sometime before 1910. (Photo: Department of Ethnology, ROM, gift of Mrs. Walter Thomas Currie)

Women and children at Chisamba mission station about 1895. The Ovimbundu had been exposed to European material culture and practices for generations, through their contact with the Portuguese. The women here are all wearing trade cloth, some made into the sort of dress preferred by the missionaries, who also encouraged their converts to cultivate the bananas seen in the background. The square shape of the house and its outdoor hearth might be further "improvements" suggested by the Canadian missionaries, who found indigenous architecture dark, smokey, and dank. (Photo: The United Church of Canada/Victoria University Archives, Toronto)

A great believer in industrial education, Currie put his faith in a carpentry shop and flour mill. He hoped these enterprises would foster not only Christianity but also legitimate commerce and what he regarded as civilized behaviour. Thus the Ovimbundu turned out flour for white bread, beds for couples to sleep in, and doors to keep their neighbours out. Female converts were to take up European dress or "modest" attire and learn how to set a table and wash dishes; in short, to become what the missionaries described as "homemakers." As well as displaying unconscious cultural arrogance and paternalism, these changes transformed the women from producers of baskets, garden foods, and pottery into consumers of soaps, spoons, and forks, while tying them tightly to the developing mission economy.

Currie believed his converts should keep their own customs, provided that these were not, in his opinion, unhealthy physically or morally. But it is unlikely he really understood how profoundly disruptive some of his "simple changes" would be. The people of Chisamba were to live, for example, in square houses of mud bricks, strung out in clearly delineated rows with carefully cultivated gardens, rather than in clusters of round, wattle-and-daub, thatched houses. These homes were to be occupied by a nuclear family composed of a man, his wife, and their children. By encouraging such living arrangements, Currie weakened alliances between lineages, discouraged the intergenerational and polygynous family, emphasized the loyalty of the couple to each other at the expense of kindred, and created a different concept of privacy.

A street, possibly Toronto Avenue, at the Chisamba mission station in Angola sometime before 1910, showing the homes of African converts. Such a street is a graphic illustration of the order and regimentation missionaries sought to impose on what they often saw as cultural confusion and social chaos. (Photo: Department of Ethnology, ROM, gift of Mrs. Walter Thomas Currie)

There were to be transformations of the inner person as well. The conversion of the man known to his people as the Lion was crucial to Currie's success. Chief Kanjundu, a life-long sufferer from bronchial asthma, went to Currie's popular medical clinic after indigenous medicine provided no relief. Converted in 1898, the chief made considerable economic sacrifices. He rejected polygyny, for example, and thereby gave up a measure of prosperity, based upon his wives' labour. He even tried to find Christian bachelors for his surplus spouses. He also freed some one hundred domestic slaves, to whom he issued documents renouncing any responsibility for their welfare or crimes they might commit. All his diviners and herbalists were driven out if they refused to convert. No beer was brewed in his capital. The Canadian missionary was particularly pleased to baptize the Lion, kneeling alongside some of his former slaves, in 1901.

All the reasons Kanjundu chose to convert cannot be reconstructed at this date, but it seems fair to assume there was a political and economic as well as spiritual alliance between the two men. Kanjundu gained preferential credit at the mission store, the right to dispense medicine from the clinic, and access to Currie's knowledge of the European world. He also saved on his tax bill, because Portuguese colonial authorities taxed African dwellings but not houses in the European style.

In 1903 Currie and his second wife Amy went on a journey into the interior, eventually travelling thousands of miles to reach Lake Nyasa. He rode an ox, while she often travelled in a hammock borne by the carriers

Chief Kanjundu about 1905, after his conversion, probably photographed by Currie, who had taken a camera with him to Africa in 1886. (Photo: Department of Ethnology, ROM, gift of Mrs. Walter Thomas Currie)

who made the journey possible. Other Africans acted as guides or interpreters and secured safe passage through different territories. After a day's march of four or five hours, the party made camp, traded cloth and brass tacks for fresh food from villages on the trail, and spent the evening singing hymns around a bonfire.

The Curries were not "eaten by cannibals," as their friends at home had feared, but returned many months later burdened with the numerous curios they had collected along the way. This trip through Zaire, Malawi, Zambia, and back into Angola, along with his pioneering evangelical work, ensured that by the time he died in 1915 Walter T. Currie was known as Canada's Livingstone.

These three objects, which offered protection against disease and misfortune, were part of a set belonging to an Ovimbundu chief, possibly Kanjundu. The beaded charm was to be worn around the neck to prevent bronchitis. Inside the pouch was a "strong medicine" for use against an enemy. The rattle was used, according to the missionary, "to awaken the spirits."

Top to bottom:
Charm, Ovimbundu, Angola, collected c. 1901. Skin, fibre, unknown substance. Height 14 cm. 901.5.31k.
Rattle, Ovimbundu, Angola, collected c. 1901. Wood, seed pods, seeds, pigmentation. Length 22 cm. 901.5.31a.
Charm, Ovimbundu, Angola, collected c. 1901. Cloth, beads, horn, fibres. Length 14 cm. 901.5.31d.
Gift of Mrs. John Currie.
(Photo: Santiago Ku)

Currie was given this staff and several head of cattle as a gift by Paramount Chief Lewanika, ruler of the Lozi people of Zambia. Also sometimes called the Barotse, these people formed one of the most powerful nations in south-central Africa. In return, the Canadian missionary offered European-style doors, tables, and beds.

Staff, Lozi, Zambia, collected before 1910. Wood, ivory. Length 85 cm. HAC428. Gift of Mrs. Walter Thomas Currie. (Photo: Santiago Ku)

The Curries collected dozens of baskets, possibly to demonstrate the basic "civility" and ingenuity of their potential converts. This set of Lunda origin may have come from the 1903 trip. They were probably used in the preparation of food crops such as manioc, millet, peanuts, beans, or maize, upon which the Lunda still depend, along with stock keeping, for their subsistence.

Baskets, Lunda, Angola or Zaire, collected before 1910. Coiled grass. *Left to right:* heights 22 cm, 33 cm, 27 cm. HAC53, HAC48, HAC56. Gift of Mrs Walter Thomas Currie. (Photo: Santiago Ku)

Unfortunately very little is known about this powerfully carved sculpture. According to the old catalogue records at the Royal Ontario Museum, Currie thought it was "used by native doctors in divining." There are no signs of wear, but one arm has been broken and repaired, which may explain why the carving was sold or given away rather than kept for indigenous use.

Human figure, Zambia, probably collected 1903. Wood, metal. Height 34 cm. HAC466. Gift of Mrs. Walter Thomas Currie. (Photo: Santiago Ku)

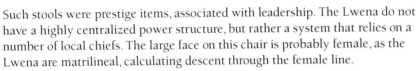

Such stools were prestige items, associated with leadership. The Lwena do not have a highly centralized power structure, but rather a system that relies on a number of local chiefs. The large face on this chair is probably female, as the Lwena are matrilineal, calculating descent through the female line.

Stool, Lwena (Lovale), Angola, collected before 1910. Wood. Height 60 cm. HAC394. Gift of Mrs Walter Thomas Currie. (Photo: ROM)

Details of carving, front and back views.

This stool was a personal gift to Emma Hostetler, a Mennonite missionary from Ontario. It was made in the Nupe kingdom of northern Nigeria, whose craft specialists were noted blacksmiths, brass workers, weavers, and tailors. Hostetler, the first worker sent out to Nigeria in 1907 by the Bethany Missionary Church, died there of smallpox in 1912.

Some gifts were probably presented because of the special status frequently accorded missionaries, who were an important source of information about the wider world. Other gifts must have been the genuine expression of friendships across cultural boundaries.

Stool, Nupe, Nigeria, collected 1907–1912. Wood. Height 9.3 cm. 983.57.6. Gift of Mr. William A. Shantz. (Photo: Santiago Ku)

The Reverend Joseph Blakeney acquired this object sometime before 1926 in what was then the Belgian Congo (now Zaire). The original catalogue entry describes the piece as an ivory god. Anthropomorphic figures are quite common in African sculpture, although portraits and statues of particular individuals are somewhat rare. Neither dolls nor decorative art but objects intimately linked to the most basic concerns of African societies, they are ideas in physical form.

This ivory figure was made for use in the Bwami association, the most powerful institution in Lega society. The source of power and legitimate authority, it provides a basis for both collective identity and action. Its members strive for the acquisition of wisdom, moral purity, and beauty, progressing through a series of ranks, or grades, of which five are for men and three for women.

Emblems of the highest male rank, carvings like this one are displayed during initiation rites. They are associated with proverbs and aphorisms outlining the moral and ethical code of the Bwami. This particular figure, called Nawasakwa Nyona, reminds the Lega, "The one who has the signs of beauty engraved on the body is no longer as he or she used to be," a comment on the transient nature of both people and things.

The patination has appeared because the figure was annointed with oil, red powder, and scent and then polished. The bodies of initiates are treated in the same way. The ivory carvings in human form are believed to have special powers in strengthening a person's life force.

Figure, Lega, Zaire, collected before 1926. Ivory, pigmentation. Height 15 cm. HA1330. (Photo: ROM)

Many missionaries returned from the field with trophies of their victories on spiritual battlefields. Most conspicuous were the so-called fetishes their converts usually surrendered. In the African context these were objects generally used for manipulating supernatural powers or attempting to mitigate their negative effects, such as the outbreak of disease or the eruption of natural disasters. But for most missionaries these artifacts were just the harmful products of pagan practices.

Writing to congregations at home about the Ovimbundu people of Angola, whom he was hoping to convert, the Reverend Walter T. Currie reminded Canadian Christians, "It is scarcely necessary to say that they are superstitious, for all ignorant people are more or less so." A great number of missionaries themselves remained more or less ignorant of African religious beliefs. Some did try to understand, and a few quite successfully, the worldviews that underpinned cultural practices like divination. But most saw diviners—whom they often called witch doctors—as competitors and denounced them.

Ovimbundu diviners determined the cause of illness, death, disaster, and misfortune, whether personal or collective. After shaking his basket, a diviner read the pattern formed by the objects, which was thought to be a message from the spirit world. He interpreted this to discover the source of the trouble that was afflicting his patients, or clients. Through various prescriptions the diviner sought to restore balance in the social order, harmony in the village, and health to the psyche or body.

This whisk was probably used to attract the spirit of a divination basket which then entered the body of the diviner, causing him to go into a trance. The Reverend Walter T. Currie described it as the property of a "fetish priest."

Whisk, Ovimbundu, Angola, collected before 1901. Horns, horse or zebra hair, reptile skin, brass. Length 71 cm. 22725. Gift of Mrs. John Currie. (Photo: Santiago Ku)

Divination basket with selected contents, Ovimbundu, Angola, collected before 1933. Woven cane, fur, feather; various materials. Diameter 18 cm. HA1840. Gift of Mrs. John Tucker. (Photo: Santiago Ku)

Leona Tucker, a missionary and the wife of Currie's successor in Angola, collected this basket sometime before 1933 from a converted diviner, who no longer needed it. Her notes on its contents help reconstruct, if only in fragments, another cultural reality.

Divination objects had specific interpretations, determined by their positions in the basket. In the selection from Tucker's basket, the human figure, for example, represented a female ancestor of noble birth, who was thought to be responsible for pneumonia, a common Ovimbundu disease. When the object appeared in association with a stool, an ancestral spirit was demanding a memorial feast. The shoulder bone of a turtle, beside the figure, was probably chosen because it looks like a woman's hoe. If it came up in the basket, the diviner told a widower to find a new wife to look after his sick children. The next object is part of a gourd, like those made into drinking cups. Its appearance meant that the spirit causing the trouble wanted an offering of beer. Representing a miniature game board, the piece of decorated ivory indicated that the trouble, whatever it was, could only be solved collectively, that is, with more than one "player." The organic tissue was a symbol for the afterbirth and suggested to the diviner that the patient was ill because it had not been properly buried, but eaten instead by an animal. The cure was a herbal infusion. The iridescent beetle, standing for the sun, announced that sickness would arrive in a few "suns," or days. An Ovimbundu proverb warns, "When the sun rises, don't whistle boastfully, for a sun holds many things in store." The colour of the piece of copper wire called to mind the reddish skin of a newborn baby. The diviner interpreted the object to mean that the person in question was an orphan, whose mother had died on the day he was born. When the small bell appeared, the diviner recalled the proverb "Even though you tie the bell inside your cloth, some movement will make it tinkle and betray you," that is, he knew that the petitioner had lied and was not telling the truth about the events under investigation.

Divination objects, Ovimbundu, Angola, collected before 1933.
Left to right:
Wood. Length 6.4 cm. HA1775.
Turtle bone. Length 5.7 cm. HA1794.
Gourd. Diameter 2.4 cm. HA1777.
Ivory, pigmentation. Length 3.2 cm. HA1798.
Organic tissue. Length 2.5 cm. HA1806.
Wood-boring beetle. Length 3.8 cm. HA1836.
Copper. Length 1.9 cm. HA1828.
Metal. Diameter 1.5 cm. HA1832.
Gift of Mrs. John Tucker. (Photo: Santiago Ku)

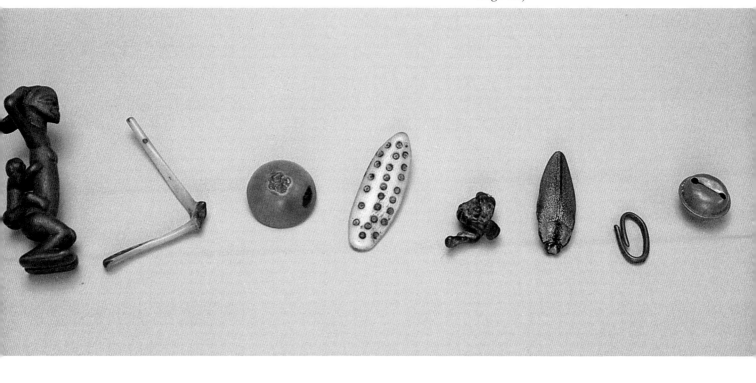

46 The Reverend T. Hope Morgan of Toronto worked with the Congo Balola Mission in Zaire from 1891 to 1911. During his long career in Central Africa, he often visited isolated Protestant mission posts by steamship, because many of the stations were on the Zaire River or its major tributaries. His collection was made during the last days of the independent Kuba kingdom, as Belgian colonial rule was being established throughout its territory.

This mask of Ngaady a Mwash belongs to one of the most distinctive masquerades performed by the Kuba people. Unfortunately the mask alone, without its richly embroidered costume, has lost some of its artistic vitality, but it is one of the earlier examples of its type collected by Europeans.

Ngaady a Mwash is the sister of Woot, the mythological ancestor, and the wife of Mwash a Mbooy, who introduced the idea of kingship. Her mask appears at both village dances and the royal court, as part of performances at initiation rituals and funerals. It is accompanied by two male masks, one of her husband-to-be and the other of his brother Mboom. The trio reenacts the events surrounding the birth of the Kuba nation and the origin of royalty, bringing the past into intimate contact with living generations.

The face painting on this mask comes from Kuba textile designs. The adornment of the piece with cloth, cowrie shells, and beads is probably an indication of the prestige and high status accorded Ngaady a Mwash in Kuba cosmology.

Mask, Kuba, Zaire, collected 1891–1911. Wood, pigmentation, cloth, beads, cowrie shells. Height 32 cm. HA2652. (Photo: Santiago Ku)

It is not known why the Reverend T. Hope Morgan collected Kuba textiles while a missionary in Zaire. He may have just appreciated their artistry or thought they provided an excellent example of the basic ingenuity and creativity of the African peoples among whom he worked and travelled.

This cloth exhibits some of the aesthetic elements that make Kuba textiles so visually exciting. A very strong rhythm is established through the combination of contrasting colours and the repetition of certain patterns, only to be deliberately interrupted by the introduction of new designs. The overall effect is one of constrained dynamism and bounded movement, much appreciated by the Kuba. While meant to be worn as clothing, these embroidered cloths, nevertheless, seem to be treated by their makers as art forms worthy of animated discussion, interpretation, and aesthetic criticism.

A Kuba cloth can only be produced through the cooperation of a male weaver and a female embroiderer. On single-heddle looms, men produce a basic plain-weave cloth from the fibres of young raffia palms, which are also dyed and used as the embroidery thread. Women choose from some two hundred designs and work their patterns without first marking them out on the cloth. Even a relatively small piece, like this one, would take at least a month to complete, the embroidery being done after the woman returned from the fields. To have the leisure time to execute these designs means that a woman belongs to a wealthy household. This in turn ensures that the cloth carries great prestige for its owner.

Detail of cloth, Kuba, Zaire, collected 1891–1911. Raffia, pigmentation. Total length 71 cm. HA2314. (Photo: Santiago Ku)

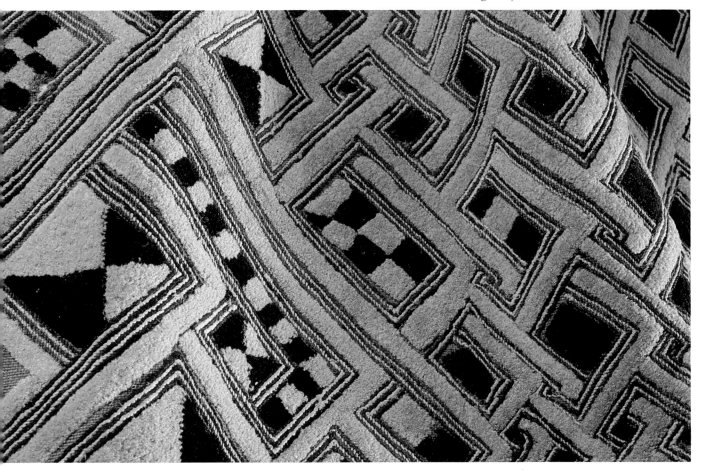

THE REVEREND A. W. BANFIELD
PHOTOGRAPHER

I had a hard job taking this photograph as the woman had to be held while I set up my camera. Just as soon as she was released and I had pressed the bulb, she ran away again. Poor creature, she thought I was going to kill her with that horrid looking thing, the camera. One cannot blame her. (A. W. Banfield, *Life Among the Nupe Tribe in West Africa,* p. 24)

The exoticism of the "Dark Continent" and its "primitive" people attracted many early photographers, some of whom were also missionaries. Unlike those who focused on the supposedly vanishing Indians of North America and tried to capture a timeless past, missionaries in Africa wanted to document the changes that their work was producing. Their favourite subjects seem to have been themselves, their evangelical activities, and church buildings. Photographs of African converts were also popular; these portraits of individuals and their families are quite different from the often anonymous group shots of the unconverted. Missionary photographs, intended to rouse the imaginations and emotions of congregations at home, illustrated lectures and publications and circulated as lantern slides and postcards.

The Reverend A. W. Banfield and his Nupe language teacher about 1903. (Photo: Courtesy of Mrs. Douglas Bryce)

Akre Mobia, a church elder from the Ivory Coast, photographed by Banfield in 1927. (Photo: Department of Ethnology, ROM, gift of the A. W. Banfield Estate)

"Mongo natives, Mompono, Congo," a photograph most likely from one of Banfield's trips for the British and Foreign Bible Society between 1915 and 1930. (Photo: Department of Ethnology, ROM, gift of the A. W. Banfield Estate)

Igbo shrine figures in Nigeria, photographed by Banfield about 1928. (Photo: Department of Ethnology, ROM, gift of the A. W. Banfield Estate)

Some of the best photographs of this kind in the collections of the Royal Ontario Museum were the work of the Reverend A. W. Banfield, who went out to Nigeria from Toronto in 1901 with the African Industrial Mission, to work among the Nupe people. A skilled linguist, he learned Nupe, eventually translated the Bible into that language, and founded the Niger Press. In 1915 he became general secretary for West Africa for the British and Foreign Bible Society. As their representative he travelled throughout West and Central Africa, covering by his own estimate some two hundred thousand miles. He reminisced later in an interview with J. H. Hunter, "In many places I walked in the very paths that David Livingstone, H. M. Stanley, and Capt. Speke and other well-known African explorers had walked in years before."

By the time ill health forced his return to Canada in 1930, he had taken over four thousand photographs. A few of them, acting as mirrors that reveal some of his own cultural assumptions as well as those of his subjects, are to be found throughout this book.

This snuff box and pipe were collected by Martha Wightman, a Canadian missionary who toured central Angola between 1917 and 1920. Tobacco was brought to Africa by European traders sometime in the 16th century. Its use became widespread, and it often had medicinal and ritual, as well as recreational, functions. In Angola, for example, tobacco leaves that had been dipped in boiling water were applied to the abdomen as a treatment for bowel inflammation or colic.

Some African peoples preferred taking snuff to pipe-smoking. The Ovimbundu, among whom Wightman travelled, thought snuff produced clear thoughts, sharper hearing, and better sight, while comforting the heart.

Both men and women smoked, a fact which seems to have particularly disturbed female evangelists. Although they disapproved of smoking, missionaries collected large numbers of pipes and snuff boxes. Some may have come from converts, who were encouraged to give up tobacco. Many of these objects provided fine examples of "native handiwork" for curious congregations at home. While utilitarian in nature, many of the pipes and boxes have great charm and appeal. The valuable metal wire on this pipe and the imported brass tacks on this snuff container indicate that they were prestige items, which both reflected and enhanced the status of their owners.

Snuff box, Angola, collected 1917–1920. Cane, tin, brass, leather. Height 10 cm. HA547.
Pipe, Angola, collected 1917–1920. Wood, iron, tin, brass. Length 53 cm. HA549.
Gift of Miss Martha Wightman. (Photo: Santiago Ku)

Although they seem to have sometimes judged each other's efforts rather critically and with an ethnocentric bias, Canadian missionaries and the peoples they hoped to convert shared an appreciation of personal grooming in general and of hairdressing in particular. Many African peoples believe that to be fully civilized a person must be properly coiffured. The details of hairstyles can reveal and confirm age, gender, social and marital status, and ethnicity. Missionaries, for their part, admired and sought to encourage the cooperation these creations required.

In his book *Life Among the Nupe Tribe in West Africa,* the Reverend A. W. Banfield noted:

> To plait a woman's hair is by no means a small task, for the hair is very thick and also very curly. A Nupe woman takes more care about the way her hair is done up than many would think. The hair is first combed out, and then a block of wood like a V turned upside down is placed on her head, and the hair is tightly plaited over this block. Should a block not be obtainable, they have learned to use old rags as a filling. When the hair is done up, it much resembles a rooster comb. There are many ways of doing up the hair, but the fashion does not change and make a certain way of doing up the hair out of date. After everything is finished, a nice cloth is used to cover the head, so as to keep out the dust. Hair done up this way will stay for over two weeks, and the trouble of doing it up every morning is done away with. (P. 40)

Nupe women dressing each other's hair, photographed by the Reverend A. W. Banfield about 1903. (Photo: Department of Ethnology, ROM, gift of the A. W. Banfield Estate)

The Reverend Walter T. Currie acquired this statue in Angola, sometime between 1886 and 1910. Its actual function and meaning or significance are unknown. The old catalogue records carefully note, however, that the hairstyle was typical for the women of Bihe, one of the Ovimbundu kingdoms.

Female figure with child, Ovimbundu, Angola, collected 1886–1910. Wood, beads, pigmentation. Height 44 cm. HAC67. Gift of Mrs. Walter Thomas Currie. (Photo: Santiago Ku)

Detail, back view.

The missionaries also collected combs and hairpins in large numbers. These objects may have been used to suggest the basic civility of potential converts and their worthiness as evangelical subjects. The high artistry of many of the combs, along with their portability, made them appealing as three-dimensional illustrations for missionary lectures and fund-raising tours in Canada.

The wooden combs and ivory hairpins illustrated were all collected

Clockwise from top left:
Comb, Angola, collected 1886–1910. Wood. Length 14.5 cm. HAC112.
Comb, Angola, collected 1886–1910. Wood. Length 11 cm. HAC113.
Comb, Lwena (Lovale)(?), Angola, collected 1886–1910. Wood. Length 15 cm. HAC337.
Comb, Chokwe, Angola, collected 1886–1910. Wood. Length 14.6 cm. HAC577.
Comb, Lwena (Lovale), Angola, collected 1886–1910. Wood. Length 18 cm. HAC339.
Comb, Angola, collected 1886–1910. Wood. Length 16 cm. HAC111.
Gift of Mrs. Walter Thomas Currie. (Photo: Santiago Ku)

between 1886 and 1910 by the Reverend Walter T. Currie during his long missionary career in Central Africa. Unfortunately, he made no distinction between ornamental and more functional combs, nor did he indicate whether the hairpins were worn by men or women. He left few records of which people actually made each piece, but most of these items probably came from Angola and seem to be of Ovimbundu, Lwena (Lovale), or Chokwe design.

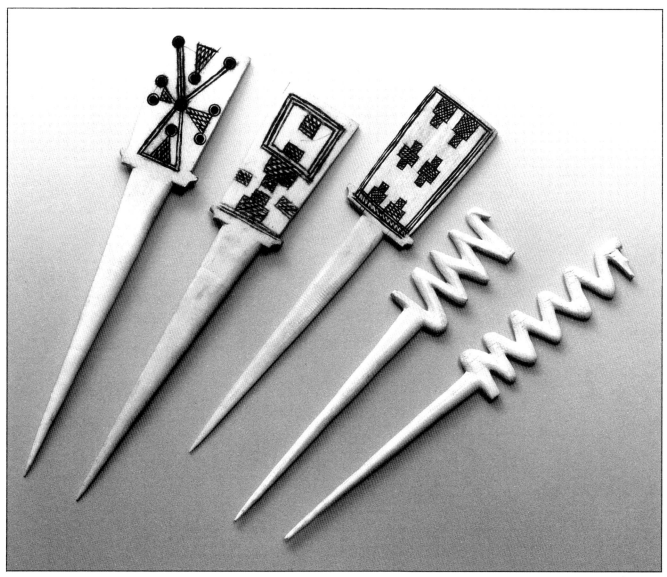

Hairpins, Ovimbundu, Angola, collected 1886–1910. Ivory, pigmentation. *Left to right:* lengths 18 cm, 18.5 cm, 17 cm, 15 cm, 18 cm. HAC117, HAC116, 944.20.31, HAC115, HAC119. Gift of Mrs. Walter Thomas Currie and Dr. Charles J. Currie (944.20.31). (Photo: Santiago Ku)

Occasionally missionaries and soldiers shared an interest in certain objects. That interest, however, may not have stemmed from the same preoccupations.

The Reverend T. Hope Morgan, who worked in the Belgian Congo (now Zaire) between 1891 and 1911, bought a large number of knives from soldiers of the Congo Free State Army. Many are of elaborate or unusual shape and fine workmanship; the throwing knife on the left in the photograph is an excellent example. Thrown so that it remained horizontal, the knife had an effective range of twenty to thirty metres. Also a hand weapon, it was carefully designed for both cutting and flying. Its general shape and decorative crosshatching suggest that it may be of Ngbaka origin. The distinctive shape of Ngbaka knives seems to have influenced the implements designed by nearby peoples.

Sometime during his missionary career the Reverend Joseph Blakeney also accumulated several knives from Zaire, which the Royal Ontario Museum acquired in 1926. He called the one illustrated an "Azande war knife," from the Uele district. Its shape, however, is more typical of Mangbetu work. These people live to the south of the Zande and are, like their neighbours, well known as metalworkers and potters.

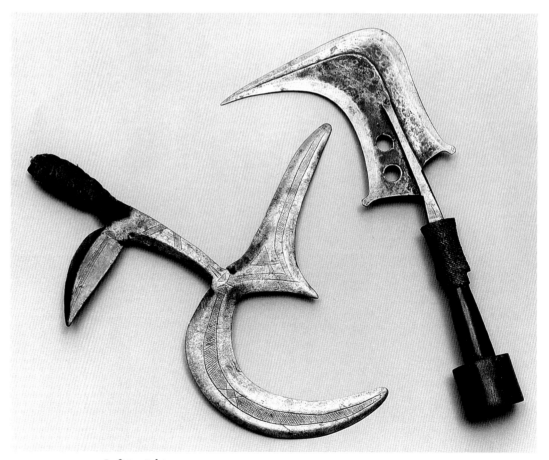

Left to right:
Knife, Ngbaka(?), Zaire, collected 1891–1911. Iron, wood, fibre, resin. Length 43 cm. HA2467.
Knife, Mangbetu, Zaire, collected before 1926. Iron, wood. Length 38 cm. HA1404.
(Photo: Santiago Ku)

Islam was first carried into North Africa by Arab armies shortly after the death of the Prophet Muhammad in the 7th century. Now found throughout the continent, it has influenced not only African worldviews and the conduct of daily life but also art and architecture. In the process Islam itself has become an African religion.

Missionaries who worked in Islamic areas hoping to convert Muslims to Christianity were often incensed by such practices as polygyny. But many were impressed with the Muslim clerics they met, whose dignity in dress and behaviour seemed more in keeping with their own standards and tastes. It was not uncommon, although far from universal, for missionaries to dress in Muslim robes, sometimes as an evangelical strategy.

The Reverend A. W. Banfield, Canadian missionary, dressed as a Nupe *mallam,* or Quranic scholar, in Nigeria about 1903. (Photo: Mrs. Douglas Bryce)

"Moslem chief and his followers," a photograph taken in northern Nigeria by the Reverend Thomas Titcombe sometime between 1908 and 1930. (Photo: Courtesy of the Titcombe family)

During the early years of the 20th century, Charles Tourney carried out mission survey work in areas of northern Nigeria that were heavily Islamicized. A selection of mementoes that he collected is illustrated. He believed that the gourd bottles "were used for Muslim prayer," by which he most likely meant that they carried the water for washing before offering daily prayers, one of the basic requirements of the faith. The string of leather amulets, or personal protective charms, is made of several small packets, each of which probably contains a piece of paper upon which is written verses in Arabic. Prayer boards were often used in teaching children verses from the Quran, the sacred text of Islam. The one shown here starts with surah 100, followed by surah 99, which is entitled "The Earthquake."

Clockwise from top left:
Bottles, Nigeria, collected in the early 20th century. Gourd, leather. Heights 18 cm, 19 cm. 969.201.14, 969.201.13. Prayer board, Nigeria, collected early in the 20th century. Wood, leather, ink. Length 53 cm. 969.201.22. Amulets, Nigeria, collected early in the 20th century. Leather, mirrors, paper(?). Length of necklace 48 cm. 969.201.56.
(Photo: Santiago Ku)

In the name of Allah, the Beneficent, the Merciful.
When Earth is shaken with her [final] earthquake
And Earth yieldeth up her burdens,
And man saith: What aileth her?
That day she will relate her chronicles,
Because thy Lord inspireth her.
That day mankind will issue forth in scattered groups to be shown their deeds.
And whoso doeth good an atom's weight will see it then, And whoso doeth ill an atom's weight will see it then.
(Mohammed Marmaduke Pickthall, trans., *The Meaning of the Glorious Koran* [New York: Mentor Books, 1953], p. 447.)

The handwoven and richly embroidered robe, shown in detail, acts as a visual statement. It reveals the wearer's profession of Islam and his allegiance to the political authority of the Muslim state known as the Sokoto Caliphate. Collected by the Reverend A. W. Banfield in the late 1920s, it is from northern Nigeria. The pattern has been identified as the one known as Eight Knives. Embroidered in cotton and silk thread, the design suggests the idea of leadership and may have offered protection during a jihad, or holy war, when originally introduced in the early 19th century.

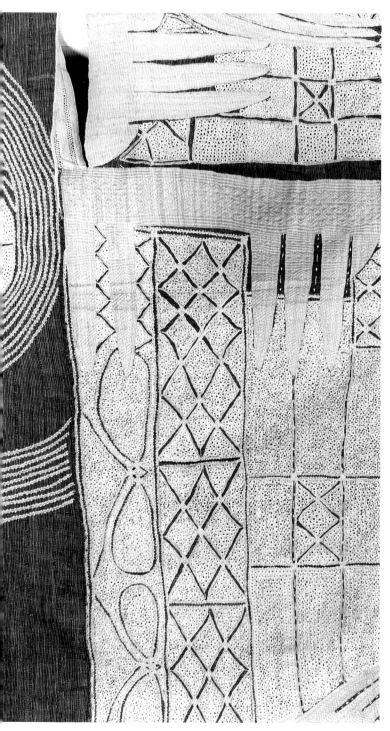

Court messengers from the Sokoto Caliphate in northern Nigeria sometime before 1930. The man on the right in the photograph may be wearing the robe illustrated. (Photo: Department of Ethnology, ROM, gift of the A. W. Banfield Estate)

Detail of robe, Sokoto Caliphate, Nigeria, collected in the late 1920s. Cotton, silk. Total length 135 cm. 950.126.2. Gift of the A. W. Banfield Estate. (Photo: Santiago Ku)

Considerable variation existed in the missionary response to African musical traditions. Drumming, for example, was actively discouraged in some places but integrated into church services in others. Missionaries themselves, however, came from a musicial subculture, for music has an important role in Christian worship in general, and hymn singing was an integral part of their Protestant evangelical services. It is not surprising that so many brought home a wide variety of musical instruments from Africa.

Often called a *sansa* or a thumb piano or finger xylophone (because of the way in which it is played), the *mbira* is one of the most common instruments south of the Sahara. An African invention, it is for the private enjoyment of its owner or may accompany communal songs and dances. Pitch is determined by the length and thickness of the metal keys. The shorter, thinner ones are high pitched, while the longer, thicker ones produce lower sounds. Young men seem to be the most frequent players of this instrument.

The *mbira* illustrated was collected sometime between 1917 and 1920 by Martha Wightman, a Canadian missionary who worked in Angola. The design on this one suggests that it may be of Chokwe origin. The metal rings at the base make a buzzing sound, which is considered an integral part of the music and complements the melody produced by plucking the keys.

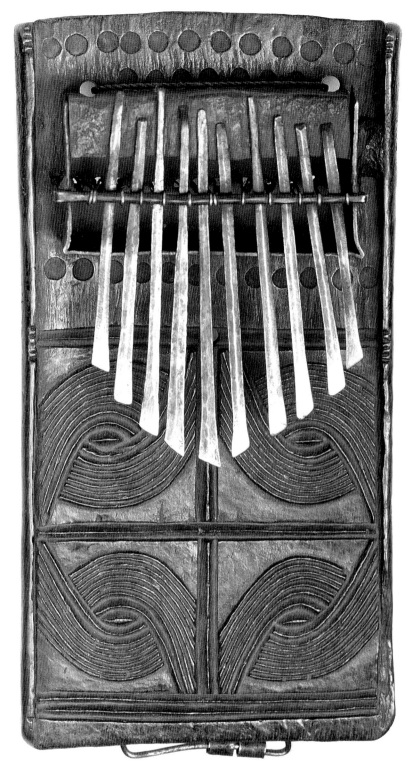

Mbira, Chokwe(?), Angola, collected 1917–1920. Wood, iron, brass, plant fibre. Length 24 cm. HA542. Gift of Miss Martha Wightman. (Photo: ROM)

Beautifully constructed stringed instruments made of a highly valued material, such as ivory, were prestige objects. They seem to have been used by professional musicians, storytellers, or diviners and were meant to accompany songs and recitations. It is also possible that elaborately decorated harps with anthropomorphic features were made for sale to colonial officials and other non-Africans. The piece shown here, collected by the Reverend Joseph Blakeney in Zaire sometime before 1926, is of Zande or Mangbetu origin. Both these groups of central African peoples were noted artisans in clay and iron, as well as ivory.

A Zande harp player, from a popular travel book of the 1870s. *The Heart of Africa,* volume 1, by Dr. Georg Schweinfurth.

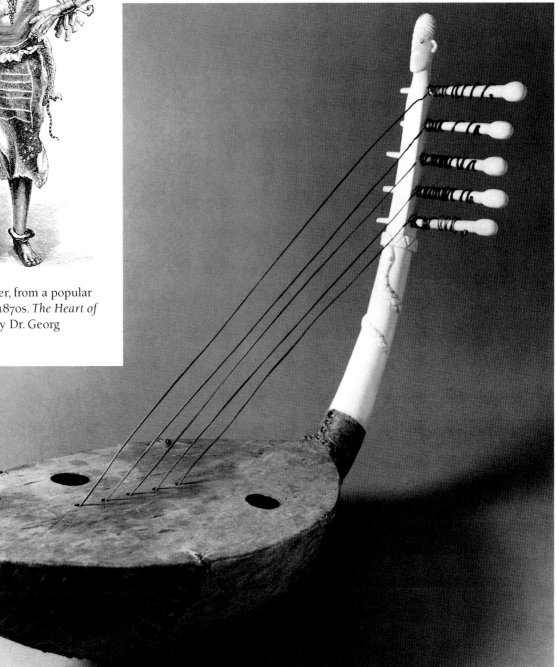

Harp, Zande or Mangbetu, Zaire, collected before 1926. Ivory, wood, rawhide, resin, beads. Length of body 40 cm. HA1316. (Photo: Santiago Ku)

DECODING COLLECTIONS

A museum collection may be thought of as a cultural text, one that can be read to understand the underlying cultural and ideological assumptions that have influenced its creation, selection, and display. Within such a collection, objects act as an expression not only of the worldviews of those who chose to make and use them, but also of those who chose to collect and exhibit them.

These objects embody relationships of many kinds: between a people and their ancestors or the supernatural world, among members of the same society, and even between groups of people separated by cultural boundaries. They materialize the ideas and concretize the categories into which all people divide the physical and cultural universe.

The earlier sections of the book examined the Royal Ontario Museum's African collections through the mind of the collector, who wished to document his or her journey into the heart of Africa. Naturally, these same collections also reveal much about the cultures of Africa: the beauty of their artistry, the variety of their subsistence patterns, the cosmological complexities of their philosophies, and the power of their political hierarchies. Finally, the nature of one of the most enduring public institutions may be better understood when the museum itself is analysed as an artifact, existing in a particular social milieu and historical period.

The lower back hall of Eldon House, home of the Harris family, in London, Ontario, sometime before 1905. Ronald Harris, a Canadian engineer, surveyed mining properties in southern Africa around the turn of the century. A hunter as well as collector, many of the artifacts and trophy heads in the photograph are mementoes of his five years travelling in Africa. The Harris and Currie families were related through marriage, and both donated African material to the Royal Ontario Museum to commemorate family achievements in what was still widely regarded as the "Unknown Continent." (Photo: Eldon House, London Regional Art & Historical Museums)

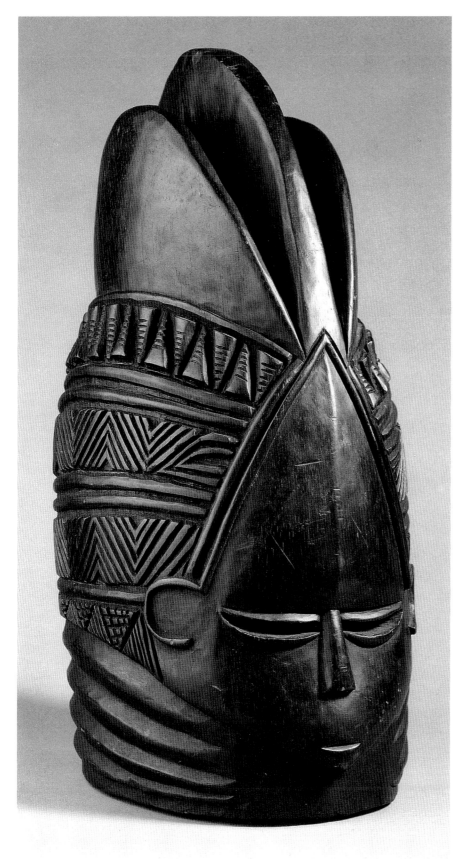

One of the most obvious characteristics of many African objects is the skill with which they were executed. The artistry that animates their forms is readily revealed.

This mask is an embodiment of female beauty. The coiffure, the high smooth forehead, the half-closed but watchful eyes, the delicately pointed chin, and the ringed neck, all speak to those who know the iconographic code of the physical and emotional composure of the mature woman. Collected sometime before 1918 by Captain A. W. Boddy, the mask was probably made in Sierra Leone.

Carved by male artists, such masks are used by the Sande society or Bundu association, to which the majority of women in Sierra Leone and the adjacent part of Liberia belong after initiation at puberty. The members of the Sande, charged with transforming children into women, teach new attitudes towards tasks already learned that will make the girls good mothers and wives. During their seclusion, initiates receive both ritual knowledge and practical advice about sexual relations, childbirth, and the rights and obligations of womanhood in general. The shiny black finish of the Sande masks reminds initiates and members alike of the river waters, home of the female spirit from whom the power of Sande comes.

The only documented case of female masking in Africa, the Sande masquerades are of considerable antiquity. They have successfully adapted to the demands of contemporary African life, in which they continue to play an important role.

Mask, Mende(?), Sierra Leone, collected before 1918. Wood, pigmentation. Height 48 cm. HA385. On loan from Captain A. W. Boddy. (Photo: ROM)

Mask, Igbo, Nigeria, collected c. 1905.
Wood, pigmentation. Height 36 cm.
976.220. (Photo: Santiago Ku)

T his fine Igbo mask from Nigeria was collected about 1905. Called *agbogho mmuo,* "maiden spirit mask," it depicts the physical and moral beauty of young girls, who are a source of both pride and bridewealth for their families. The elaborate hairstyle and facial tattoos are drawn from real life. White, prominent on the face of this mask, is the colour of the supernatural world, particularly of ancestors, and signifies goodness. Masks like this one are still owned collectively and used by male age grades, appearing at celebrations and the funerals of important people. The men who wear the masks base their dance steps on those of young women.

Although the mask or headdress is the piece most frequently collected and displayed in a museum, it is one part of a performative whole, which might include not only costume and choreography, but music, the singing of the spectators, the heat and dust of the dry season, and the charged atmosphere of the festival itself.

An Igbo dancer from southern Nigeria, photographed about 1928 by the Reverend A. W. Banfield. (Photo: Department of Ethnology, ROM, gift of the A. W. Banfield Estate)

African artistry is not confined to works meant for the glorification of chiefs, appeals to the supernatural, and the honouring of ancestors. It is found as well in more mundane objects, items often meant for personal adornment and private pleasure.

The striking colours and patterning of these beaded gourds suggest that they were made by Xhosa women living in South Africa in the early years of the 20th century. Skilful beading and aesthetic judgement have transformed what were probably containers for perfume, snuff, or medicine into strongly appealing art forms.

Containers, Xhosa(?), South Africa, collected before 1916. Gourd, beads, fibre. *Left to right:* heights 18 cm, 15 cm. HA755, HA752. Gift of Trinity College, University of Toronto. (Photo: Santiago Ku)

African pastoralists, although they often keep sheep and goats, are best known as cattle herders. Cattle, whose blood and milk are more important as food than their flesh, are the primary form of wealth in many East African cultures. The ownership of large herds brings power as well. These animals are used in the completion of social contracts and the payment of bridewealth and sometimes in religious rituals as sacrifices. Indeed, many of the rhythms of social life are determined by the needs of the cattle, which are often the focus of creative or aesthetic attention.

The Maasai rely on young warriors, armed with buffalo hide shields and well-polished spears, to defend the family herds from human and animal predators. The shield and spear pictured here were collected in 1909, although it is not known if they were found in Kenya or Tanzania.

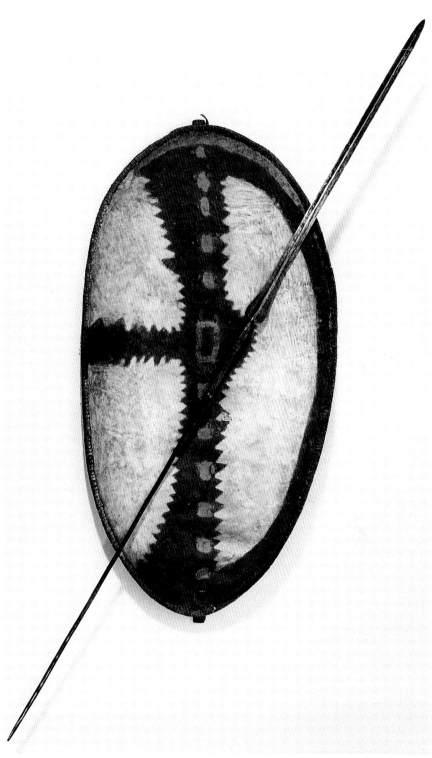

Shield, Maasai, Kenya or Tanzania, collected before 1909. Hide, wood, pigmentation. Length 130 cm. HA52.
Spear, Maasai, Kenya or Tanzania, collected before 1909. Iron, wood. Length 200 cm. HA19.
(Photo: Santiago Ku)

68 Along with the hunting and gathering of wild foods and the herding of animals, horticulture provides the third basic subsistence pattern found in Africa. The social and ritual lives of farmers dependent on crops vulnerable to a host of natural and human disasters are intimately tied to the agricultural seasons.

The Ovimbundu word for "year" comes from the verb meaning "to cultivate." And it is with hoes like the one illustrated that Ovimbundu women care for the maize, or corn, which is the main staple of their diet. Introduced by the Portuguese from Brazil, maize replaced millet or sorghum, perhaps as early as the 17th century. At the time this hoe was in use at the end of the 19th century, each woman had not only her own house but also her own fields and granary to store her harvest.

This hoe was collected by the Reverend Wilberforce Lee of Cowansville, Quebec, who worked with the Canadian Congregational Church in Angola between 1889 and 1895. He never acquired a taste for the local cornmeal porridge. Writing home in 1889 from somewhere on the trail, he complained, "We were fortunate to-day in being able to purchase some sweet potatoes and young onions, and these made a valuable addition to our evening meal of mush. Native mush is *not* the most palatable thing in the world, but still we *can* eat it, and we have to do so every night."

Hoe, Ovimbundu, Angola, collected 1889–1895. Iron, wood. Length of blade and handle 60 cm. 973.325.16. Gift of Miss Dorothea Bell. (Photo: Santiago Ku)

Everything from seashells to salt functioned as a medium of exchange in Africa, but the use of metal was particularly widespread. Metals were important in the transactions completing social contracts. Durable, relatively portable, and easily measured, they could also be transformed into weapons, tools, and ornaments, which added to their value.

These copper ingots, sometimes called Katanga crosses, served for centuries as signs of wealth and standards of value. They formed part of bridewealth payments and had to be returned to the bride's family if the marriage failed. It is said that in 1910, along the Kasai River in Zaire, one such cross would buy five or six chickens, two lengths of good cloth, three or four kilograms of rubber, or six axes. Cast in sand moulds, these ingots have a rough finish. They were all once in the collection of the Reverend Walter T. Currie.

Clockwise from top:
Ingot, Zaire, collected 1886–1910. Copper alloy. Length 20 cm. HAC376. Gift of Mrs. Walter Thomas Currie.
Ingot, Zaire, collected 1897. Copper alloy. Length 18 cm. 16860. Gift of Mrs. John Currie.
Ingot, Zaire, collected 1886–1910. Copper alloy. Length 18 cm. 944.20.6. Gift of Dr. Charles J. Currie. (Photo: Santiago Ku)

Masks, Yoruba, Benin, collected before 1924. Wood, pigmentation. *Left to right:* heights 30 cm, 28 cm. 924x9.73, 924x9.2. (Photo: Santiago Ku)

The complexities of African worldviews find expression not only in the abstractions of living beliefs and the rhythms of daily life, but also in material form, in objects. These Yoruba masks represent two female priests wearing ritual headdresses. Although Gelede masks are worn by men, the masquerades celebrate or acknowledge the spiritual powers of elderly women and female deities and ancestors, known collectively as "our mothers." The dance is meant to ensure that these powers are harnessed for the benefit of society and do not find expression in antisocial practices and disastrous events. The "children," that is, the Yoruba people, offer the performances to please and placate their "mothers." Missing here are the veils that cover the dancers' faces and the layers of cloth that disguise their bodies.

The masks appear in pairs at large public festivals held during the afternoon in the marketplace, before the rains begin, to mark the new agricultural season. There are male and female masks, and each gender has a distinctive choreography. Several characters drawn from Yoruba life are portrayed, some favourably and others negatively. Prostitutes, market women, traders, Muslim clerics, and strangers from other ethnic groups are among the various types represented.

This set of Gelede masks was collected sometime before 1924 in Dahomey (now Benin). The serene expressions, which are common in this kind of mask, are still appreciated by Yoruba audiences.

A young Nigerian woman, probably Yoruba, photographed sometime before 1930 by the Reverend A. W. Banfield. (Photo: Department of Ethnology, ROM, gift of the A. W. Banfield Estate)

Female figure with child, Yombe,
Angola or Zaire, collected before
1924. Wood, mirrors, pigmentation.
Height 57 cm. HA848. (Photo: ROM)

The Yombe, part of the great Kongo group of peoples, made figures, such as this mother and child, as funerary sculpture. Their graves, particularly those of village elders, leaders, or family heads, were marked by these effigies, which usually featured the dead person, a spouse, or occasionally an attendant. A small shelter or shrine on the grave housed the figure, which was thought to offer aid or comfort to the deceased. The facial streaks are sometimes identified as tears.

Collected before 1924 on the west-central coast of Africa, this figure is wearing a chief's cap, what may be a leopard-tooth necklace, and armlets, all of which indicate a person of some rank or social standing.

"Mongo Wives Mourning for Deceased Husband at Mompono, Congo," a photograph by the Reverend A. W. Banfield taken sometime before 1930 in what is now Zaire. To the caption he added, "The women cover their bodies with white clay and mourn for many days." (Photo: Department of Ethnology, ROM, gift of the A. W. Banfield Estate)

74 This type of Kongo sculpture, called *nkisi nkonde,* is frequently described as a nail fetish, but is better understood as a power figure. Rather than being owned by an individual, it was probably used collectively, to protect the community and attack those who sought to do the villagers harm. Such objects played an important role in the procedures for swearing oaths, determining guilt or innocence, and exacting revenge, although this particular figure's precise functions can no longer be determined.

The carver began by making a plain statue; a ritual specialist added magical or medicinal ingredients, which in this case are hidden behind the mirror inset in the stomach. Mirrors in such pieces were said to turn evil aside and throw it back upon those who seek to propagate misfortune. The nails were driven in during use, to arouse the figure to action or to mark events, such as the conclusion of a treaty. This figure seems to have had quite an active career, to judge by the number of nails, spikes, and blades embedded in it.

Missing the spear or staff that was in its upraised arm, this sculpture was collected in west-central Africa sometime before 1924. The Kongo, a large group of peoples who share linguistic and cultural traits, are found in Congo, Zaire, and Angola.

Power figure, Kongo, Angola or Zaire, collected before 1924. Wood, iron, clay, resin, pigmentation, glass, mirror. Height 64 cm. HA847. (Photo: ROM)

African leaders, from village headmen to the rulers of large centralized states, were often associated with objects that clearly defined and enhanced their secular and spiritual powers. The fly whisks pictured here were employed on state occasions. They are political power expressed in physical form. Such objects continue to be symbols of authority in many African societies, where they are widely used by elders, chiefs, kings, and presidents. These whisks were collected between 1884 and 1886 by a Canadian doctor, Rolph Lesslie, in what is now Zaire.

Whisks, Zaire, collected 1884–1886. Cane, copper. *Left to right:* lengths 80 cm, 82.5 cm. HA461, HA462. Gift of Mrs. I. W. Lesslie. (Photo: Santiago Ku)

"Chiefs of Egbe visiting mission house on Christmas morning," a photograph taken sometime between 1908 and 1930, from the album of the Reverend Thomas Titcombe, who worked in northern Nigeria. An added note calls attention to the umbrellas "used *only* by chiefs." (Photo: Courtesy of the Titcombe family)

istinctive hats and headdresses are one of the most common ways to distinguish rank and political leadership in Africa. This Kongo chief's cap was an emblem of his power, influence, and authority in both the secular and spiritual realms. It is adorned, very appropriately, with the teeth and claws of a leopard, an animal often associated with African rulers. The Reverend T. Hope Morgan acquired this piece in what is now Zaire, sometime between 1891 and 1911.

A Yoruba chief wearing a beaded crown and veil, photographed in Nigeria by the Reverend A. W. Banfield in 1925. (Photo: Department of Ethnology, ROM, gift of the A. W. Banfield Estate)

Cap, Kongo, Zaire, collected before 1911. Pineapple fibres, leopard teeth, claws.
Height 12 cm, diameter 18 cm. HA2357. (Photo: Santiago Ku)

78 Often displayed on ceremonial occasions and sometimes on social ones as well, chiefly regalia make the leader the focus of any public event and reminds everyone of both the rights and obligations of political power. This beautifully carved staff was collected by the Reverend Walter T. Currie during his long missionary career in Central Africa. Currie seems to have been attracted to, and perhaps was given in large numbers, various sorts of staffs. Some were simply part of the formal attire of most adult men and are often of inferior carving. Others were executed with great skill and imagination. This staff was probably displayed as an emblem of rank or wealth, and may have also functioned as an insignia of office.

Staff, Angola, collected 1886–1910. Wood, brass. Length 105 cm. HAC594. Gift of Mrs. Walter Thomas Currie. (Photo: Santiago Ku)

Detail, side view.

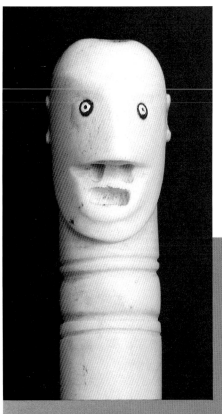

P restige items usually exhibit exceptional artistry and are sometimes made from rare or especially valued materials. Ivory, for
example, is particularly valued throughout Central Africa. Its use
in these horns made by the Zande suggests that they belonged to or were
played for a person of high rank. The transformation of elephant tusks
into musical instruments was accomplished with great skill.

Detail of HA973.

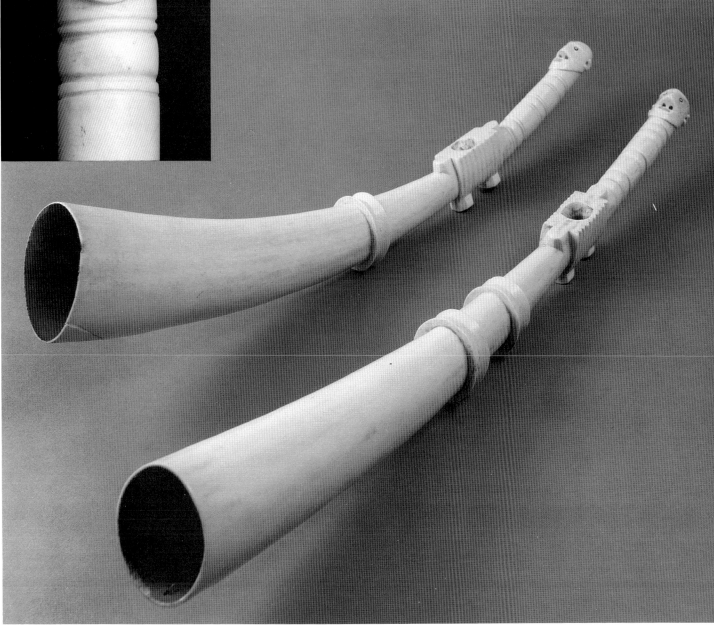

Horns, Zande, Zaire, collected before 1926. Ivory, resin, beads. *Top to bottom:*
lengths 48 cm, 53 cm. HA973, HA1328. (Photo: Santiago Ku)

Museums are often accused of being cultural charnel houses, full of the remains of dead civilizations. Sometimes there has been an element of truth in the allegation. Primitivism has induced a certain predilection among collectors for some mythical culture in a pristine state. In the past, ethnographic curators were most concerned with the difficult task of trying to reconstruct another cultural reality through its objects. An uncritical emphasis on traditional culture and an aboriginal or precontact past helped promote a picture of an unchanging society.

This is not always an easy situation to correct. The core of the African collections at the Royal Ontario Museum is made up of objects amassed in the last quarter of the 19th century and the first quarter of the 20th. As such, the collections are historical, and it is impossible even to suggest through these objects the complexities of contemporary African life at the end of the 20th century. What one can do, however, is realize that the lifeways of all peoples change; no one lives in a collective state of suspended animation.

Two very creative responses to change can be seen in the objects illustrated here. The Mangbetu or Mamvu pot from Zaire features a woman with an elaborate coiffure. These peoples considered an elongated skull a sign of beauty, and it was produced by binding the head soon after birth. Anthropomorphic vessels of this kind were produced for a very short period, beginning about the same time as Belgian colonial rule. The presence of Europeans stimulated a demand for particular kinds of objects,

"Preparing a Meal, Matadi," a photograph by the Reverend A. W. Banfield taken sometime before 1930. Matadi was an important town on the Congo (now Zaire) River, and there is much evidence here of cultural change. Most obvious are the European-style clothing and the gun; it is much harder to deduce these people's worldview from their material culture. (Photo: Department of Ethnology, ROM, gift of the A. W. Banfield Estate)

Pottery vessel, Mangbetu or Mamvu, Zaire, collected before 1926. Fired clay. Height 24 cm. HA1379. (Photo: Santiago Ku)

82

A Ngombe elder from Zaire, photographed by the Reverend A. W. Banfield sometime before 1930. (Photo: Department of Ethnology, ROM, gift of the A. W. Banfield Estate)

including figurative pots. They seem to have functioned not only as prestige items within Mangbetu society, but also as chiefly gifts to foreigners. Some pots may have been commissioned directly by non-Africans from artists participating in the growing cash economy in the region. For that reason, the person who made this example was most likely a man, although women usually made all the household ceramics. The Reverend Joseph Blakeney collected this piece sometime before 1926 in the Belgian Congo (now Zaire). The Mamvu are part of the large Mangbetu cluster of related peoples in this area.

This Ngala or Ngombe chief's stool, also from Zaire, shows another response to social change. Carved with a sure hand, this piece of furniture is also a wonderful sculpture. What were mundane brass tacks in a European context have taken on a totally unexpected vitality when imported and used in an African one. The Reverend T. Hope Morgan acquired this piece between 1891 and 1911 during his missionary career in Central Africa.

Stool or chair, Ngala or Ngombe, Zaire, collected 1891–1911. Wood, brass. Height 43 cm. HA3008. (Photo: Santiago Ku)

M any objects are in museums because their exoticism appealed to the original collector. The "barbarity" of other people's customs, whether alleged, witnessed, or just imagined, was often a powerful incentive. By acquiring such an object, collectors could concretize a cultural chasm or demonstrate their own unquestioned assumption of cultural superiority at the top of some imagined evolutionary hierarchy.

The original catalogue entry for this headdress states that it was "bought from one of the cannibal tribes in the Azumini market." Its collector, Jabez Elliott, a Canadian doctor who worked in southern Nigeria in 1900 and 1901 with an antimalaria expedition, further described it as a "warrior's hat."

Headdress, Igbo(?), Nigeria, collected c. 1900. Fibre cords. Width 25 cm. HA2735.
Gift of Mrs. Charles P. Holmes. (Photo: Santiago Ku)

Museums are sometimes charged with cultural vandalism, represented by their collections of decontextualized objects, far removed from their original setting and meaning. A corollary is the often-voiced fear that to be the focus of the collection process is a symptom of cultural decline. To single out particular museums or individual collectors is probably unfair. Museums are themselves social institutions, which cannot be divorced from the historical context in which they developed, and their collections occasionally reflect the violence and disruptive social forces characterizing the European colonization of Africa.

John F. Crean's reasons for collecting these goldweights are unknown, but he acquired them while in Ghana as a captain in the Gold Coast Regiment of the West African Frontier Force, during the campaign of 1900 against the Asante people. Since the 18th century, their kingdom had been one of the most powerful of the Akan states. Its economy rested on the exploitation of gold, which was the basis for domestic and international trade. Taxes, death duties, and fines were also paid in this metal. The Asante developed an ingenious weighing system for their gold dust. Based on a combination of Islamic and European standards, it used brass counterbalances that were often, as here, in geometric form. The brass for

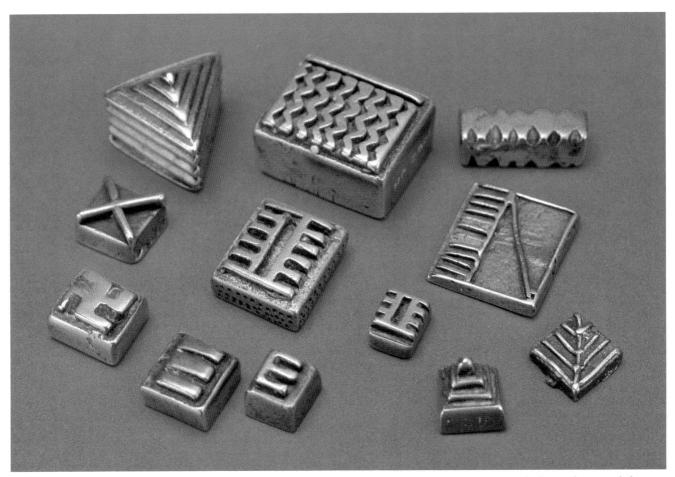

Goldweights, Asante, Ghana, collected c. 1900. Brass. *Clockwise from top left:* lengths 2.3 cm, 2.8 cm, 2.5 cm, 2.5 cm, 1.2 cm, 1.1 cm, 1.1 cm, 1.9 cm, 1.1 cm, 1.2 cm, 1.3 cm, 1.3 cm. HA2021, HA2001, HA2020, HA2019, HA2023, HA2015, HA2012, HA1997, HA2009, HA2004, HA2000, HA2022. On loan from the Royal Canadian Military Institute, Toronto. (Photo: Santiago Ku)

making the goldweights, which were all cast by the *cire perdue* method, came either from the north across the Sahara or from the southern coast, where Europeans imported it in large quantities.

Crean may have acquired his goldweights from the followers of the chief of Bekwae, an Asante ruler who allied himself with the British. Or they may have come from Asante who resisted. In any event, a series of Anglo-Asante power struggles and wars throughout the 19th century had disrupted not only the political system but the economy as well. By the end of that century, these goldweights were probably more important as curios for sale to soldiers than as part of an active currency system.

The accidental or serendipitous nature of many museum collections is obscured when exhibitions with clearly distinguished "storylines" and carefully developed sequences of cases impose a unity on a miscellaneous collection of objects. The pipe in the photograph, for example, might be selected for an exhibition on the culture of the Lala people of Zambia, or for one comparing tobacco and smoking paraphernalia around the world. Nevertheless, it was not collected for those reasons.

In 1903, while working with the Congregational Church mission in Angola, the Reverend Walter T. Currie chose not to go home on furlough, but decided to see some of his friends at other missions and to visit African peoples living in the interior. Gone for many months, he travelled thousands of miles, eventually reaching Lake Nyasa, crossing through the same territories explored by Dr. David Livingstone many years before. Currie acquired several pipes, although not as illustrations of an ethnographic point or as pieces of material culture for examining social practices. For him they were a very particular kind of memento, because he bought them "from a native close to where Dr. Livingstone died."

Youth smoking a gourd pipe, probably photographed about 1903 by the Reverend Walter T. Currie in what is now Zambia. (Photo: Department of Ethnology, ROM, gift of Mrs. Walter Thomas Currie)

The partiality of museum collections has sometimes promoted stereotypes about other cultures of a rather limited nature. This has happened to the Zulu people of South Africa. The warrior image was an important part of Zulu cultural identity, but the disproportionate number of their weapons in museum collections has obscured the many other facets of their collective existence.

While there are several reasons why such a situation evolved, a key element was undoubtedly the battle of Isandhlwana in January 1879, which made the Zulu one of the best-known and most-feared African peoples in the British Empire. A twenty-thousand-strong Zulu army annihilated a column of the invasion force, killing hundreds of British soldiers and uncounted numbers of their African allies. This massive defeat of white by black sent shock waves throughout the empire.

Fighting without artillery or cavalry against both African and European foes, the Zulu employed an attack formation that took the shape of a charging bull. The large "horns" were formed by the younger regiments, who ran out and encircled the enemy. The "chest," which made the heavy

"Lord Beresford's Encounter with a Zulu." *The Illustrated London News,* 6 September 1879.

THE ILLUSTRATED LONDON NEWS.

REGISTERED AT THE GENERAL POST-OFFICE FOR TRANSMISSION ABROAD.

No. 2099.—VOL. LXXV.   SATURDAY, SEPTEMBER 6, 1879.   WITH WHOLE SHEET SUPPLEMENT   SIXPENCE. By Post, 6½d.

frontal attack, was composed of battle-seasoned warriors. The reserves, or "loins," sat with their backs to the battle until called in to finish off what remained of their opponents. This style of attack helped the Zulu establish and maintain one of the most powerful indigenous states in southern Africa. But it was, in the end, ineffective against European entrenched positions and gunfire.

Self-defence was thought cowardly by the Zulu. The shield, while it did protect the body, was intended as an offensive weapon for hitting or unbalancing the enemy. The white colour of the shield in the photograph reveals that it belonged to a married man, a veteran in an older, experienced regiment. Zulu herdsmen used spears of various sizes and shapes when hunting and defending their herds. In battle most men had at least two spears, the extras being carried by the young boys who accompanied the army with food and sleeping mats. The knobkerrie was a club for striking opponents at close range. This particular example came from the collection of one of Britain's most well known soldiers, Field Marshal Horatio Herbert Kitchener.

The Zulu reputation as a warrior people probably accounts for the large number of their spears, clubs, and shields now filling museum storerooms. Many of the soldiers who fought against and eventually defeated the Zulu brought home trophies to celebrate their own survival and victory. Later collectors, seeking a vicarious thrill from a quickly romanticized past, bought uncritically of anything offered for sale as a Zulu weapon. These and other "primitive" weapons were often displayed in late Victorian homes of the middle and upper classes. This was the next step in their transformation from weapon to war trophy to decorative art, and finally, to museum exhibit. The objects in the photograph are displayed in a typical 19th-century European arrangement.

Shield, Zulu, South Africa, collected before 1909. Hide, wood. Length 116 cm. HA853.
Spears, Zulu, South Africa, late 19th century. Iron, wood, cane. Lengths 152 cm, 137 cm. HA34, HA23.
Knobkerrie, Zulu(?), South Africa, late 19th century. Wood. Length 60 cm. 948.1.35. Gift of Lord Kitchener Estate.
(Photo: Santiago Ku)

Art critics, scholars, collectors, and curators frequently categorize certain objects as primitive art. What were masks, shrine sculptures, and ancestral figures have been taken from their original cultural context and put into another. With emphasis sometimes on their aesthetic qualities and at other times on their ethnological content, these objects are labelled, displayed, and sold as art forms and artifacts. This process can be seen in the history of the Royal Ontario Museum's African collections. Many of the pieces were first acquired as curios, later as ethnographic specimens, and occasionally, as in this case, as art.

Made by the Kota people of Gabon, sculptures like the one illustrated were intended by their creators as reliquary guardians. They were attached to baskets holding the skull or bones of distinguished ancestors. Probably grouped together in a shrine, they protected the relics from witchcraft and received sacrifices meant to ensure that the villagers lived long, healthy, and prosperous lives.

The oval faces of these figures are usually concave and surrounded by sculptural elements, which may represent elaborate coiffures. The copper and brass in this piece were the products of European trade. Both rare and expensive, they were thus deemed appropriate materials with which to honour the ancestors.

The semiabstract treatment of the human body in these reliquary figures made a powerful impact on several European artists who were to become part of the modernist movement. By the time this piece was offered to the Museum in 1924, it was no longer referred to as an ethnographic artifact, but very carefully described as African art. Collected by a Colonel Georges François Bois, probably a French colonial administrator, it was being sold by Auguste Leblond, who was described in Museum records as "a prominent art critic in Paris."

Reliquary guardian figure, Kota,
Gabon, collected before 1924. Wood,
brass, copper. Height 64 cm. 924x9.8.
(Photo: ROM)

Plaque, Edo, Nigeria, 17th century. Leaded brass. Height 43 cm. HA352/1. (Photo: ROM)

Museums sometimes compete with each other in their acquisitions, and collections often come to resemble each other, as certain kinds of artifacts come into fashion. Such has been the case with the Benin Bronzes, as they are collectively known. They caused a public sensation when first seen in Europe at the very end of the 19th century. Part of that interest was generated by the spectacular circumstances in which the objects were acquired.

For centuries Benin City had been the capital of one of West Africa's most successful precolonial states, when it fell in 1897 to a British punitive expedition. Much of the city and the huge wooden palace of the *oba,* or king, was burned. After the capture of the town, several hundred leaded brass plaques were removed. Some were later sold by the Admiralty to help recoup the costs of the campaign.

Probably dating from the 17th century, these plaques were originally attached to wooden pillars in the palace, where they documented the triumphs of the *oba*'s empire and illustrated the complexities of daily life at his court. The figure on this piece is almost certainly a retainer in that court. He wears a headdress or beaded cap and a loincloth, has what may be a bell hanging from a sash across his chest, and carries a sword tucked under his arm. Four stylized crocodile heads mark the corners of the plaque. Symbols of power, they were the favourite sacrifice to Olokun, god of the sea.

The appearance of these objects on the European market was sudden and dramatic. Mostly representational in nature, the art was in accordance with European tastes of the period. The great skill required to cast the plaques was recognized, although it was sometimes erroneously attributed to non-African craftsmen. Easily understood, the subject matter was made more compelling by its exoticism and association with what British newspapers reporting on the punitive expedition called the "City of Blood." Today the Benin Bronzes are some of the most expensive African pieces offered for sale on the international art market.

EPILOGUE

By studying the museum as an artifact, reading collections as cultural texts, and discovering the life histories of objects, it has become possible to understand something of the complexities of cross-cultural encounters. In the same process, the intricacies of different cultural configurations are revealed in objects through which various African peoples have expressed not only their individual artistry but also their deepest communal concerns. Finally, by placing in context the relationships, however brief, problematic, and painful, that developed as Canadian soldiers and missionaries travelled into the heart of Africa, it has become clear that the past is part of the present.

Riverscape in Zaire, photographed by the Reverend A. W. Banfield sometime between 1915 and 1930. (Photo: Department of Ethnology, ROM, gift of the A. W. Banfield Estate)

Adams, Monni. "Kuba Embroidered Cloth." *African Arts* 12(1): 25–39, 106–107 (1978).

Agthe, Johanna and Karin Strauss. *Waffen aus Zentral-Afrika.* Frankfurt: Museum für Völkerkunde, 1985.

Asiegbu, J. V. J. *Nigeria and Its British Invaders 1851–1920.* New York: NOK Publishers International, 1984.

Banfield, A. W. *Life Among the Nupe Tribe in West Africa.* Berlin, Ontario: H. S. Hallman, 1905.

Banta, Melissa and Curtis M. Hinsley. *From Site to Sight: Anthropology, Photography, and the Power of Imagery.* Cambridge: Peabody Museum Press, 1986.

Barker, H. W. *The Story of Chisamba.* Toronto: Canada Congregational Foreign Missionary Society, 1904.

Barthorp, Michael. *The Zulu War: A Pictorial History.* Poole: Blanford Press, 1980.

Bastin, Marie-Louise. "Lwena: Arts of the Angolan Peoples." *African Arts* 2(2): 46–53, 77–80 (1968).

———. "Tshokwe: Arts of the Angolan Peoples." *African Arts* 2(2): 40–46, 60–64 (1968).

———. "Mbundu: Arts of the Angolan Peoples." *African Arts* 2(4): 30–37, 74–76 (1969).

Bebey, Francis. *African Music: A People's Art.* New York: Lawrence Hill, 1975.

Biebuyck, Daniel. *Lega Culture: Art, Initiation, and Moral Philosophy among a Central African People.* Berkeley: University of California Press, 1973.

Biebuyck, Daniel, and N. Van den Abbeele. *The Power of Headdresses.* Brussels: TENDI, S.A., 1984.

Ben-Amos, Paula. *The Art of Benin.* London: Thames and Hudson, 1980.

Bingham, R. V. *Seven Sevens of Years and a Jubilee! The Story of the Sudan Interior Mission.* Toronto: Evangelical Publishers, 1943.

Boone, Sylvia. *Radiance from the Waters: Ideals of Feminine Beauty in Mende Art.* New Haven: Yale University Press, 1986.

Bravmann, René. *African Islam.* Washington and London: Smithsonian Institution Press and Ethnographica, 1983.

Brett-Smith, S. "The Doyle Collection of African Art." *Record* (Princeton University Art Museum) 42(2): 1–45 (1983).

Brincard, Marie-Thérèse. *The Art of Metal in Africa.* New York: The African-American Institute, 1982.

Buel, J. W. *Heroes of the Dark Continent.* Toronto: Historical Publishing Company, 1890.

Celenko, Theodore. *A Treasury of African Art from the Harrison Eiteljorg Collection.* Bloomington: Indiana University Press, 1983.

Chernoff, John M. *African Rhythm and African Sensibility.* Chicago: University of Chicago Press, 1979.

Cole, Herbert, and Chike Aniakor. *Igbo Arts: Community and Cosmos.* Los Angeles: Museum of Cultural History, UCLA, 1984.

Cole, Herbert, and Doran Ross. *The Arts of Ghana.* Los Angeles: Museum of Cultural History, UCLA, 1977.

Cornet, Joseph. *Art of Africa: Treasures from the Congo.* London: Phaidon Press, 1971.

———. *Art from Zaire.* New York: The African-American Institute, 1975.

Cribb, Joe. *Money: From Cowrie Shells to Credit Cards.* London: British Museum Publications, 1986.

Currie, W. T. Papers and Correspondence, 1886–1910. United Church of Canada Archives, Toronto.

Dark, Philip. *An Introduction to Benin Art and Technology.* Oxford: Clarendon Press, 1973.

de la Haye, Sophie. *Tread upon the Lion: The Story of Tommie Titcombe.* Scarborough: Sudan Interior Mission, 1974.

Drewal, Henry and Margaret Drewal. *Gelede: Art and Female Power among the Yoruba.* Bloomington: Indiana University Press, 1983.

Einzig, Paul. *Primitive Money.* London: Eyre and Spottiswoode, 1949.

Fagg, William. *Nigerian Images.* London: Lund Humphries, 1963.

Fagg, William and John Pemberton. *Yoruba Sculpture of West Africa.* New York: Knopf, 1982.

Fagg, William and John Picton. *The Potter's Art in Africa.* London: British Museum Publications, 1970.

Fraser, Douglas and Herbert Cole. *African Art and Leadership.* Madison: University of Wisconsin Press, 1972.

Freyer, Bryna. *Royal Benin Art.* Washington: Smithsonian Institution Press, 1987.

Fry, Jacqueline. *Visions and Models.* Kingston: Agnes Etherington Art Centre, Queen's University, 1984.

Garrard, T. F. *Akan Goldweights and Gold Trade.* London: Longmans, 1980.

Hamilton, F. "Rough Notes on Native Tribes of South Africa." *Archaeological Report* (Ministry of Education, Legislative Assembly of Ontario), 1900:40–49.

Haywood, Colonel A., and Brigadier F. A. S. Clarke. *History of the Royal West African Frontier Force.* Aldershot: Gale and Polden, 1964.

Hommel, William L. *Art of the Mende.* Baltimore: University of Maryland Art Gallery, 1974.

Hunter, J. H. "A Light Bearer in Darkest Africa: The Amazing Story of A. W. Banfield." *The Evangelical Christian,* February 1950, pp. 78ff.

Idiens, D. *The Hausa of Northern Nigeria.* Edinburgh: Royal Scottish Museum, 1981.

James, Lawrence. *The Savage Wars: British Campaigns in Africa 1870–1920.* London: Robert Hall, 1985.

Jenkins, Jean. *Man and Music.* Edinburgh: Royal Scottish Museum, 1983.

Jones, G. I. *The Art of Eastern Nigeria.* Cambridge: Cambridge University Press, 1984.

Kecskési, Maria. *African Masterpieces from Munich.* New York: The Center for African Art, 1987.

Kennedy, Carolee. *The Art and Material Culture of the Zulu-Speaking Peoples.* Los Angeles: Museum of Cultural History, UCLA, 1978.

Kriger, Colleen. "Robes of the Sokoto Caliphate." *African Arts* 21(3): 52–57, 78–79, 85–86 (1988).

Lamb, Venice. "Cloths of the Gold Coast." *Hali* 41:16–25 (1989).

Laufer, B., W. Hambly, and R. Linton. *Tobacco and Its Use in Africa.* Leaflet 29. Chicago: Field Museum of Natural History, Chicago, 1930.

Maquet, J. *The Aesthetic Experience.* New Haven: Yale University Press, 1986.

McLeod, M. D. *The Asante.* London: British Museum Publications, 1984.

Meurant, G. *Shoowa Design: African Textiles from the Kingdom of Kuba.* London: Thames and Hudson, 1986.

Monti, Nicolas. *Africa Then: Photographs 1840–1918.* New York: Knopf, 1987.

Morris, James. *Heaven's Command*. New York: Penguin, 1979.
——. *Pax Britannica*. New York: Penguin, 1979.
——. *Farewell the Trumpets*. New York: Penguin, 1979.

Neyt, François. *Traditional Art and History of Zaire*. Brussels: Société d'Arts Primitifs, 1981.
Nitecki, Andre. *Equal Measure for Kings and Commoners*. Calgary: Glenbow Museum, n.d.
Nketia, J. H. K. *Music of Africa*. New York: W. W. Norton, 1975.
Northern, Tamara. *The Art of Cameroon*. Washington: Smithsonian Institution Press, 1984.
——, ed. *Expressions of Cameroon Art: The Franklin Collection*. Rembrandt Press, 1986.

Olaniyan, Richard, ed. *African History and Culture*. Lagos: Longman Nigeria, 1982.

Paudrat, J. L. *The Way of the Ancestors*. Paris: Éditions Dapper, 1986.
Perrois, Louis. *Ancestral Art of Gabon*. Geneva: Barbier-Mueller Museum, 1985.
Phillips, Ruth. "The Iconography of the Mende Sowei Mask." *Ethnologische Zeitschrift Zürich* 1:113–132 (1980).
Picton, John, and John Mack. *African Textiles*. London: British Museum Publications, 1979.
Preston, George N., and Polly Nooter. *Sets, Series and Ensembles in African Art*. New York: The Center for African Art, 1985.

Roy, Christopher. *Art and Life in Africa*. Ames: University of Iowa Art Museum, 1985.

Schildkrout, Enid, J. Hillman, and Curtis Keim. "Mangbetu Pottery: Tradition and Innovation in Northeast Zaire." *African Arts* 22(2): 38–47, 102 (1989).
Schweinfurth, Dr. Georg. *The Heart of Africa,* volume 1. London: Sampson, Low, Marston, Searle & Rivington, 1878.
Sieber, Roy. *African Textiles and Decorative Arts*. New York: Museum of Modern Art, 1972.
——. *African Furniture and Household Objects*. Bloomington: Indiana University Press, 1980.
Sieber, Roy, and Roslyn Walker. *African Art in the Cycle of Life*. Washington: Smithsonian Institution Press, 1987.

Thompson, Robert Farris. *African Art in Motion*. Los Angeles: University of California Press, 1974.
——. *Black Gods and Kings*. Bloomington: Indiana University Press, 1976.
Thompson, Robert F., and Joseph Cornet. *The Four Moments of the Sun: Kongo Art in Two Worlds*. Washington: National Gallery of Art, 1981.
Tucker, J. T. *Drums in the Darkness*. Toronto: Doran, 1927.
——. *Currie of Chissamba*. Toronto: United Church of Canada and Ryerson Press, 1945.
Tucker, Leona. "The Divining Basket of the Ovimbundu." *Journal of the Royal Anthropological Institute of Great Britain and Ireland* 70:171–204 (1940).

Vansina, Jan. *Art History in Africa*. London: Longman, 1984.
Vogel, Susan. *For Spirits and Kings: African Art from the Paul and Ruth Tishman Collection*. New York: Metropolitan Museum of Art, 1981.
——. *African Aesthetics, the Carlo Monzino Collection*. New York: The Center for African Art, 1986.

———. *Perspectives: Angles on African Art.* New York: Abrams and the Center for African Art, 1987.

———, ed. *Art/Artifact: African Art in Anthropology Collections.* New York: The Center for African Art and Prestel Verlag, 1988.

Vogel, Susan, and F. N'diaye. *African Masterpieces from the Musée de l'Homme.* New York: Abrams and the Center for African Art, 1985.

Volavka, Zdenka. *Hidden Treasures from Central Africa.* Downsview: Art Gallery of York University, 1973.

———. *Dialogues: African Sculpture from Toronto Collections.* Downsview: Art Gallery of York University, 1975.

———. "Insignia of Divine Authority." *African Arts* 14(3): 43–51, 90–91 (1981).

Wardwell, Alan. *African Sculptures from the University Museum, University of Pennsylvania.* Philadelphia: Philadelphia Art Museum, 1986.

Westerddijk, P. *The African Throwing Knife.* Utrecht: University of Utrecht Press, 1988.

Wittmer, Marcilene, and William Arnett. *Three Rivers of Nigeria.* Atlanta: The High Museum of Art, 1978.